School-Dazed
Parents

School-Dazed
Parents

Charles S. Mueller

SAINT LOUIS

Copyright © 1994 Concordia Publishing House
3558 S. Jefferson Avenue, St. Louis, MO 63118-3968
Manufactured in the United States of America

Library of Congress Cataloging-in-Publication Data

Mueller, Charles S.
   School-dazed parents / Charles S. Mueller.
      p.3f cm.
   ISBN 0-570-04667-x

   1. Child rearing—United States. 2. Child rearing—Religious aspects—Christianity. 3. School children—United States. 4. Parenting—United States—Public opinion. 5. Teachers—United States—Attitudes. I. Title

HQ769.3.M85 1994

649'.1—dc20   94-13042

---

1 2 3 4 5 6 7 8 9 10   03 02 01 00 99 98 97 96 95 94

To the many elementary schoolteachers, special guardians of our children during the formative years, who willingly gave so much to the content of this book.

CPH Books by Charles S. Mueller

ALMOST ADULT

THE CHRISTIAN FAMILY PREPARES
FOR CHRISTMAS

LET'S TALK

THEN COMES THE BABY
IN THE BABY CARRIAGE

Contents

Preface
Getting Started

◆

This is not a book for children. It's for parents. Not just one kind of parent. *All* kinds of parents: single parents, parents of blended families, traditional, nuclear-family parents, rural parents, East-Coast/West-Coast parents, North and South too. Parents of all colors and cultures. And any other kinds of parents that might come to your mind.

While all parents fall within my general concern, this book does have a tighter focus. It is specifically prepared to help moms and dads who are caring for children between the ages of four and 12. But there's also advice for parents of kids younger and older than that age range. (I'll tell you more about it a little later.)

I said help. That's all. This is not a road map to the Kingdom of Perfect Parenthood—as if there were such a place! No wildly unrealistic parental idealism here. All I want to do is help real, live parents be effective within the limits of their personal gifts and their life circumstances. Nothing more than that. But nothing less either.

Is it possible to enhance parental effectiveness? To answer that question I asked hundreds of pastors to identify parents whom they believe are effective. Their task was easy. They sent me names of hundreds faster than I thought possible. Statistically that means there are thousands of them out there. Effective parents are not rare. They are modest though. With no exception, they were surprised someone would see them as effective. These remarkable people believe that what they do can be done by anyone willing to make the effort. Based on their testimony—testimony that I believe—you can become much more effective than you now are. I promise.

Promise? How can a promise of improved effectiveness be made in the face of the massive parental failures that personal experience and newspaper reports identify every day? Easy.

First of all, those who are irretrievable parental disasters will not be reading this book. (Now *there's* a word of comfort for you who are even now scanning these words!) They won't hear my promise, understand its power, or yearn for improvement. They lack, or have stifled, any desire to improve their parenting skills. Don't ask me why. I don't know. I could only guess. But I don't know how to help them.

Still, I wish we could do something for their poor children.

Their children, deprived of constructive help at home, will bear the burden of parental ineffectiveness all their lives. My heart goes out to them—and my hand as well. Could you and I compact together to help them? It's worth a try. I've talked with some who have become wonderful parents in their turn. They did it with the model of a friend's family or through the tutoring of a great spouse.

The second reason I can promise increased effectiveness is that it has such a wonderfully wide-ranging connotation. It's not a tight, task-oriented term, limited by precise, objective criteria. It's more relational than duty bound. There are wonderfully effective inner-city parents, blind parents, single parents, parents who never passed the eighth grade, even learning-disabled parents. Some are athletic and others are not; some are musical and others are tone deaf; some are articulate while others mostly smile and listen; some have money while others have almost none. They come in all styles. Your style too.

But in this way they are identical: They yearn to be the best possible parents for their children. Do you want that? If you do, then you can be effective.

School-Dazed Parents is one of a three-book series, linked by a concern for parental effectiveness. The opening book in the series, *Then Comes the Baby in the Baby Carriage,* (CPH, 1994), focuses on a child's earliest years. It derives much of its uniqueness from the comments, observations, insights, suggestions, and opinions of hundreds of effective parents whom I sought out and questioned. Their explanations of effective parenting are both instructive and inspirational to me. *They* are the ones who convinced me that parental effectiveness is achievable.

There were also hundreds of others I talked with while preparing the first book who weren't so sure they could attain effectiveness. They were first-time parents, nurturing children aged one day to about four years. After meeting and interviewing them, I compared their comments with my pool of proven effective parents. Good news! It would be only a matter of time before the younger parents would catch up with their more experienced predecessors. All they needed was a few more experiences. The companion title for this book, *Then Comes the Baby in the Baby Carriage,* can be called upon as the grass-roots text book for Parenting 101. It parallels and underpins this book. The rudiments of effective parenting are spelled out there—together with suggestions for making them your own.

The third book in this series will also zoom in on effective parenting—only the focus will be on parenting during the teen years, those exciting years of sudden and wondrous change/change/change. Count them. There are three substantial and magnificent shifts in those seven years. They happen so fast that if a mom and dad aren't paying attention, they may find enormous life events will blur, like a roller coaster that is known for its ups and downs and its breathtaking speed.

One more thing: Neither this book, nor the other two, contain secret formulas for parental effectiveness. No long lost entrances to the world of productive parenting. To be truthful, after checking years and years of literature on parenting, I found there has been little written on the subject for generations. Maybe even centuries. So what's the point of *School-Dazed Parents?*

While much in this book is no newer than common sense and the content of many well-known parenting publications, the way data was gathered and connected is brand new. Just the fact that they are built on verbatim insights of hundreds of effective parents makes all three books unique. *School-Dazed Parents* has an additional element. I interviewed elementary schoolteachers on your behalf asking them, "Based on your experience with children, what are the things parents could do at home to help their children grow, mature, and succeed in life?"

What also emerged for me was a sense of urgency. There are a frightening number of dysfunctional families in our world. Teachers are forced to deal with them through their students. They are in our neighborhoods. While this book is not about dysfunctional families, their problems intrude into our homes and urge us to offer informed assistance. Ineffectiveness is infectious, and if we are not careful, dysfunctionality will become the norm. We need to help the good get better and the better stay that way—all the while offering help to ineffective moms and dads. If not to them, then their children.

As you read this book, make it unusable for anyone else—unless that "anyone else" doesn't mind reading a book that is marked up, underlined, and scribbled in the margins. Read with a pen or pencil in hand. Make notes for yourself. Jot down examples from your experience that confirm a point made here or there.

And if you disagree with something? Write that, too, so you can think it through in the light of all you read later. If you wish to write me about either pluses or minuses, I'd like that. I promise to answer your letters if I can, but in any case to share your work with others whenever and wherever I speak.

May I make another suggestion guaranteed to bless you? Discuss this book with someone else. Your spouse for sure. A friend, yes. A class or maybe a little group, certainly. If you create a small group, try to include a few moms or dads whose parenting moment is different from yours. They will help you talk through tough topics. And, of course, invite some whom you see as effective parents. If you aren't sure who that might be, I'll give you clues in a later chapter. For now, weigh the qualities of those who parent around you and invite some whom you feel model your ideals. Don't be surprised if they are surprised to be asked. Their surprise is one of the sure signs that you have picked right.

Parenting is a wonderful subject for an adult group. Everyone has something good to offer, if they will. Even commonplace advice and inferior examples are instructive. Group discussion helps you establish your personal baseline to fashion your parenting skills. In talking with others you'll be better able to evaluate yourself. And it's a wonderful way to pass on some of the helpful experiences you have had without appearing to be giving unsolicited advice.

Bottom line? Don't miss your moment to learn. Decide now to take some steps toward improvement. You will never regret it. Your children will never forget it.

Now it's on to the world of effective parenting under the promised blessing of God.

Natural Consequences

No one could be more surprised at the subject matter of this first chapter than I. I didn't really choose it. It just spilled out onto the paper, almost of its own volition—so different from what I had in mind when I first measured this book. But that can't be helped. *They* would have it no other way.

"They" are the elementary schoolteachers I listened to in the search of important things effective parents ought to know and understand. They pushed it right up to the head of the line and said it had to be discussed first. This placement was not so much a matter of intentional decision as it was one of unconscious emphasis.

Theirs was not a lone voice. Grade-school-age children, upon reflection, agreed with their teachers and told me so. The smaller ones couldn't always fully define this theme, but they spotted it for what it was as soon as they saw it. In talks with teens, they underlined the importance of this chapter with identical intensity but in more detail than their younger brothers and sisters could muster. And lots of parents, some who could be called good (even others not so good), kept flitting toward, and around, this point, until the heat of the subject matter overwhelmed them.

One of the odd things about this first emphasis is that it wasn't number one on anyone's inventory of what's important in effective parenting of elementary-school-age children. Every segment came up with something different in the top spot. But this matter was present, and quite high, on everyone's list. The subject? *The importance of helping children face natural consequences.*

Facing natural consequences. A Christian teacher, after spending 30-plus years in the classroom—most of it in public education—has this to say about natural consequences in the life of a child:

> *There are many parents who want to "rescue" their children from the natural consequences of their actions. If their child does not do an assignment, the parents will write lengthy notes explaining why their little Johnny didn't have time to do his work, when, in fact, he didn't want to. When they begin doing this at a very early stage of a child's education, the child grows up believing that Mom/Dad*

will write a note, or come up with an excuse, whenever they wish. And the child will understandably take advantage of this. Once the parental rescuing cycle begins, it is hard to break.

Lest you dismiss her comments as that of a bitter teacher (she's not) or with a sniffy but-that's-public-education-for-you, her Christian day school counterparts say the same thing, with equal intensity—many in much greater detail.

I love those warning words: "rescuing children from natural consequences of their actions." That teacher's phrasing is irony in the extreme, so gritty with reality you can almost feel it. And is she ever right! There *are* natural consequences in life, sure as the ultimate whump of a bucket that has slipped from your hand as you are going down the basement steps. Once released, gravity—a natural consequence—takes over.

Isn't it heartening that teachers want to tell parents about the danger of misconceived rescue attempts? If they didn't, I surely would. Some days I seem to spend most of my time tending folks who are trying to evade the natural consequences of their life decisions rather than deal with them. No way! Even if I *could* help them do what they want, I wouldn't. Understanding and dealing with natural consequences is essential to achieving the full life.

They teach indispensable lessons. The earlier we pass life's class in natural consequences (we never graduate from it!) the quicker we can be on our way toward maturity.

Is "facing natural consequences" too harsh an expression for you? It seems to be for some. How about a softer one, such as "dealing with cause-and-effect." Better? Or we might substitute even gentler phrasings, such as "recognizing normal reactions," or "handling expected responses," in the place of the steamier "natural consequences." That's okay. Go ahead. Words aren't what's important here. What's important is helping parents teach their children the direct and inescapable relationship between what the child does and the consequences she/he faces based on their actions.

So where shall we start with the primary concern? How about with something obvious: Both parent and child must recognize it is possible to mask the natural consequences of an action, and that such masking helps neither parent nor child. Worse. It leaves the child ignorant of life's normal responses to flawed behavior. And, just as bad for the adults, it sets up the parent for a deeper hurt later. There is a sure and certain day when an outside force will not (or cannot) be brought to bear by parents in time. On that day, the day the parental cavalry charge does not get there in time, the evaded earlier lesson will finally be taught. When I grew up in Kansas during the '30s, that lesson had a name. It was called "learning the hard way."

Let me give two examples of what interfering with natural consequences at the elementary-school level can look like. Both actually happened. The names have been changed to protect the guilty.

At 10 years of age, Billy went out for the ball team. He was not very good. How could he be? He didn't really practice. He didn't try hard either. But Dad was determined Billy would make the team ... and play. He was always there to "protect" Billy. He hounded the coach so that the coach would leave Billy in for situations Billy could not really handle. Dad sniped at the umpires. After a while, they would rather walk Billy than call a third strike and listen to you-know-who. That's how Billy bumped along in sports, exerting minimum effort, honing few skills. Not a bad deal! He always played, was in the team photograph, and coasted from league to league until ...

At 13, Billy went out for a team whose coach wasn't intimidated by Billy's dad—in a league that threw curves. Bye-bye, Billy. Only now Billy was no longer 10. He was a teenager whose fragile sense of self was always threatened. From all sides. Billy didn't need more rejection, deserved or undeserved. But he got it anyway. And there wasn't a thing Dad could do about it. Or Billy.

Too bad, Billy. Who knows how good of an athlete he might have been? Or whether his horrid teen years might have turned out differently.

Another story? Sure.

Yvonne was not a very popular eight-year-old. She was demanding. She was rude. She always wanted to be stage center. Children her age didn't like her and would not have invited her to their parties—except for her mom. Her mom could smell out a party or a sleepover with the efficiency of a bloodhound. She'd get Yvonne invited to events. How? She pressured other moms. Yvonne grew up disadvantaged. Her "helpful" mom spared her the need to make important adjustments in life. Result? She was as impossible a person at 18 as she had been at eight, only now the world in which she was involved included dating, college, and summer jobs—and life. When she finally "learned the hard way," Yvonne moved to another city away from her mom. And Mom was left to tell the whole world (or anyone who would listen) about her ungrateful child, "for whom I did everything."

True story? A *common* true story.

I often address teachers' conferences. When I ask them what other teachers classify as the number one problem of parenting, there's usually a little guessing and lots of quizzical looks. When I start talking about children who are shielded from natural consequences, the interest is stirred and I'm often interrupted with laughter and applause. Neither is for me. They are responding to the identification of such a universal difficulty that it's almost unnoticed. And *then* the teachers start telling their own stories of parents who write deceiving notes or carry on dishonest conversations to cover a child's mistake. If you're not sure the point of this chapter is real, ask a teacher.

But why would parents do this to kids? Why would they lie about things that have such great potential for teaching life's basic and often most important lessons?

I can't offer every reason, but a few call out for recognition.

- There are parents whose own sense of worth is so wrapped up in their child they seem unable, or unwilling, to differentiate between their own life and that of a son or daughter. Their son must make the team. Their daughter must get the lead in the play. Their child may not fail, even when the child has little interest in the parent's goals. This is not normal. Their hope for, and joy in, their child's accomplishments is not natural. Theirs is a hunger for their child's success that they long to absorb into themselves. And failure? Unthinkable! Carried to extreme, they might even attempt murder so that their daughter could become a cheerleader. An absurd thought? Read the newspaper. It happened.

- There are parents who believe their children are so fragile that they must be spared any pressure for fear they might break. Stories about overly protected little-rich girls, spoiled heirs, and pampered children are abundant and offer ample evidence of this point. And, it's not new. Long ago, royalty reportedly had whipping boys for their children. When the child misbehaved, the whipping boy was punished. Beyond imagination? Not hardly. I'm sure that if whipping boys were legal today, there would be a market—or at least rentals.

That's enough about overly protected kids or bad parents. The subject is too depressing. Besides, this book isn't for or about *in*effective parenting. I want to help parents who are effective recognize their blessing and hang on to their standards. I also want to help any who want to improve. My only interest in mentioning the negative examples is for recognizing that it exists and that it needs to be handled. So, let's get to that.

And let's start at the top with a fact: Parents have a purpose, the primary one is that of teacher of truth and example of all that's better in life. Those roles are not superseded by providing food, shelter, and protection for the child. To the contrary. Providing food, shelter, and protection is a subset of teaching truth by serving as a positive example.

The home is not primarily a fort or retreat center or escape. Its primary function is as the child's first, and most important, school. It's where all the basics of life are to be taught with Mom and Dad as the primary faculty. That's why ineffective parents are so dangerous. They fail to teach the correct lessons in the first and most important educational institution of life, the one to which all other schools in life are subordinate. While it is possible to learn many of life's lessons elsewhere, the task is tougher— like learning about English from a German-speaking instructor. It's the home, with Mom and Dad as the faculty, reinforced by the rest of the family, by their circle of friends, by their church, and by all the other agencies in their lives, where learning how to face life's natural consequences is best and most easily taught. Even if I, personally, were not sure this is true, I'd come to believe so based on the witness of two elementary schoolteachers. To them the home is the most elementary of elementary schools.

A second-grade teacher writes: *The home is the ideal place to encourage your child. It is there parents can teach that even wrong decisions are learning experiences that can be turned to good—if the educational moment is not missed by parent-teachers who refuse to teach.*

A fifth-grade teacher urges: *Talk about the decisions your child makes, particularly those that get them into trouble. Help them to understand and accept their action, and grow from it. Teach them.*

See why I like the teachers I consulted? They are understanding, right to the point. These two represent the kind of well-organized common sense I found in the comments and suggestions of so many elementary school-teachers. The opinions of the three teachers cited so far suggest the need for a kind of basic, key course: "Thinking in Life's Key Moments 101." And what might that course's content contain? I picked up these elements from the comments of perceptive teachers.

- At or near the center of every critical moment in life there is a moment, a flicker in time, when the actor has a chance to evaluate possible steps or consequences. Children need to know about that moment and that it is surely coming to them. Consider Eve who held the fruit in her hand for a moment before the first bite. (Gen. 3:6 describes the sequence in slow-motion language: "When the woman saw that the fruit of the tree was good for food and pleasing to the eye, and also desirable for gaining wisdom, she took some and ate it.") Children will have those same moments of teetering between right and wrong, before either is chosen. God talked to Cain about all that in Gen. 4:6–7. Search out God's "fatherly" teaching moment and see how he handled it with the first family. Things haven't changed.

- The older the child becomes, the more complex and consequential life's decisions. In the earliest years a child is taught how to make decisions by rules that take the place of a thinking process: "Don't touch the stove when it is hot" or "Never run with scissors in your hand." In time those rules are so internalized that they are reflexive. That happens quicker and easier if the parent-teacher clearly explains the reasoning behind the rule *and outlines the natural consequence*. Sometimes, sad to say, the explanations have to be repeated after an accident has happened.

- Wise parent-teachers spell out things, in detail, even when the circumstance might justify immediate and unquestioning obedience. "Because I told you, that's why" is a parental response of very limited value and must be followed up later with a lot more detail. Children, even the youngest, need and can understand a reasoned explanation. They may not agree with it, but they can understand it.

- Every moment has educational potential. The home school is always in session. Talk to your children. Then listen to them. Encourage feedback. Note the times and places they did the right things. That's positive reinforcement. Take the time to determine whether your important message got through. All that parent-teacher conversation will, at the very least, reinforce the lesson that might be learned. This process turns an event, good or bad in itself, into learning. And learning is what life at home is all about.

How early should a parent start the intentional educational process? As early as possible. Certainly long before their child's elementary school days. In *Then Comes the Baby in the Baby Carriage* an entire chapter presents what effective parents have to say about the school-in-your-home and its importance. You can teach even the smallest ones the why and how of dealing with natural consequences. How? Play "What If" with the children.

Ask them, "Okay, what if I let you stay up until 10 and you don't get enough sleep tonight?" Talk about it. Or, "What if I did your homework, as you asked, and let you watch TV?" Let them reason their way through questions like that. Make it a game. Give them time to develop their best response. Don't hurry the process. Don't let feelings get in the way of their answer. The "right" answer is of little long-term value if the process for developing it is not understood. Start that game early in a child's life and keep playing it. The issues they face get more complex with every passing year. Initiate your own Head Start program in your home.

A second element you will want to teach at the school-in-your-home is deciding. Decide means "to cut." When you decide, there is no turning back. That's why learning how to cut well, or decide, is a critical skill in life. Making the right cut the first time is a key growth skill. If you skimp on the cut, or chop off less than needed, that doesn't mean you have escaped consequences. Oh, no. It means you'll have to cut again. The dress with too much hem gets cut again. A 2" × 4" cut one inch too long will meet the saw a second time. And don't forget. You'll do the sawing. Effective parents look for ways to help their children learn how "to cut"—to decide— and how to do it right.

But how? Easy. Let them make decisions, good or bad, right from the start. When Grandma sends your daughter $5 to spend as she wishes, effective parents let her do just that. They, of course, give advice but then mask feelings as the child works through the process of making choices. Instead of telling her what to buy, allow her to work her way through the process until she comes to a decision that she can and does claim. Is there an exception to this approach? Yes. *The parent steps in when physical danger is involved.* Otherwise the decision lies with the child.

And if she spends the $5 on something dumb? A poorly managed $5 is a cheap price to pay for the child learning a lesson about money management. So say effective parents. In the long run the educational goal is to help the child develop lifelong values. A value is nothing more than a decision consistently and publicly claimed in one of life's important areas. The parental goal is to teach the child how to establish values by making decisions and while learning to deal with natural consequences. See how it works?

Do children make good decisions from Day 1? Hardly. If they did, what would be the point of the school-in-the-home? Some kids always make safe decisions and need to be taught how to take risks. Life is more than a series of safe decisions. Others seem drawn to erratic and uneven choices. They need to be taught principles of consistency. Still others are reckless and will profit from lessons in judgment. All will make mistakes. The first goal is not so much learning how to avoid mistakes as learning how to manage them once they've happened. The effective school-in-the-home is a wonderful place for translating "mistakes" into lessons for life—with minimum scar tissue. That will happen *when* a patient parent who understands the teaching/learning process is determined to be effective as well.

And what do you do with mistakes? Ignore them or excuse them? No, not at all. You work with them. Sometimes in the earliest home years every son or daughter will make a conspicuously inferior decision, one you could have spared them if you had been more directive. Instead of a tidy correction you have a mess on your hands—one *you* could have prevented. That's not bad. You have a moment for teaching the truth about consequences.

Instead of yelling at a son or daughter, or freezing them with disdain, teach. Try to help the child see that there were choices. They could have asked the advice of consultants, advisors, or friends. Advice that is sought and followed before the fact can spare a lot of later grief. For the moment forget the specifics. Ignore the skinned knee, or the bent bicycle, or the lost marbles. Go for the educational gold. Help them see the lesson to be learned—the upside of a downer. A small loss today could prevent a major catastrophe later *if you snatch the potential victory from the jaws of what many see as defeat*. Who wouldn't want to teach that to a child?

Lest you underestimate the power in the previous paragraph, isn't that how you, as an adult, make good decisions today? Don't you consult *Consumer's Guide,* or seek advice from a specialist or competent friend before you make a purchase? And don't you try to determine which stores are reliable and what product lines are well-tested before you make a purchase? And didn't you learn to do that after a series of failures you'd like to forget? *That* can and ought be taught in the home. You can teach your child to seek guidance and support when making life's decisions. It's less likely that you'll have to rescue your child from natural consequences if you have an educational plan in place to help them learn for life. A start? Point out where good, basic, user-friendly support can be found. Audie and I did that with our children. How? We took them to one of life's great sources of advice, the Holy Bible, and treated it as such. We built modern life applications on the Bible stories we read to our kids and on the Sunday school lessons they were learning.

The Bible is not only the source of salvation's story—its primary purpose—but a great guide in life as well. We worked hard at helping our children learn how to apply God's truths to specific life circumstances. You can do the same. There are appropriate stories for almost every situation. If you don't feel equipped to teach the Bible one-on-one, work with them through guides such as *Almost Adult* (CPH, 1993), a devotional book for children ages 9–11. You also can open their eyes to the fuller possibilities of the church and the many spiritual guides available in times of decision. The pastor, a teacher, a youth worker, or a deaconess are all ready to support in times of decision. If you aren't comfortable doing all the teaching yourself (and who is?), call on those resources to give you a hand. They'll do that with joy.

Oh, yes, it won't take the thinking child long to learn the value of advice from brothers and sisters—and good friends. It will take them even less time if you, as parent, help them understand the potential in those sources. All you really have to do is pose these local "experts" as possibilities, and let the child discover the value of your suggestion. Later, on their own, they'll discover that the circle of care gets larger and larger as life goes on. The home is the place where those understandings are taught best—by effective parents who are ready to help their child face life's natural consequences.

And one more important home lesson: Recognize and commend grit and determination in your children. It's a comparatively short step in life from a child's decision to take piano lessons to their sitting at the piano at a party, playing for the others—*if they hang in there*. It's an even shorter step from digging a garden to gathering luscious tomatoes or plucking beautiful flowers for *those who keep at it*. Hobbies, projects, and commitments all fall within the world of thinking/deciding/evaluating *and persisting*. Help your children develop true grit by teaching them the importance of persistence. Your child's paper-route decision, or his starting a community lawn-mowing business decision, or her promise to feed and water any puppy that might show up at the house every day decision are important settings for teaching the value and importance of thinking/evaluating/deciding/persisting.

The proven, effective parents whom I will introduce in chapter 5 have some helpful hints on how all this happens. Their common sense suggestions include these three:

- Teach by *word* and *deed,* with the word explaining the deed and the deed illustrating the *word.*

- This (and almost everything else of value in the world of parent-child relations) is best done one-to-one, in private.

- The most helpful style of teaching is positive, nonpejorative reinforcement. Truth is not taught very well if the student is demeaned. Never call your child names. The shamed child doesn't hear well. And the shaming parent doesn't make much sense.

May I emphasize again that this book is not intended to correct a seriously dysfunctional family? There are experts (and it takes an expert) who are trained to help crippled families. Some may suggest extreme methods such as *tough love*. But that kind of treatment is not for the normal family. In the normal family, that would be like doing brain surgery for a skinned knee. Instead, a loving, steady-handed approach helps children through the life stages that have enough tension without introducing excessive parental responses. If you feel "more" is needed, use the same approach that you would suggest to your son or daughter: Seek expert advice.

A last thought about the home: It is the greatest classroom in the world where wondrous mysteries can be studied, great truths can be explored, thrilling experiments can be conducted, and the secrets of life can be shared. It happens best one-to-one. One-to-one teaching has unbelievable power for communicating great truths, not only in ideas but in the teacher's tone, expression, intensity, and warmth. Standing right there, the teacher can "read" the student and be poised to respond to every question and curiosity.

The teacher must be very careful not to quench the spirit. Out of curiosity, children can ask all kinds of odd questions. If you aren't able—or ready—to answer, say so and set some time in the future when you will be ready. Be very careful that a "different" kind of question is not categorized as dumb or wrong. Questions may be premature or inappropriate or too complex. You can say that. But take care that a negative comment about the question does not bleed over to the questioner. It's such a short step from being told a question is dumb to feeling like you are dumb.

Instead, reinforce the child by honoring his question, "That's a great question to ask" or "You certainly have a keen eye for observation." Commendation, public or private, is great. Don't hesitate to use positive reinforcement. If children receive enough natural affirmation from you, they won't have to beg for it from another.

Of course, affirmation must be honest and true. Even with that rigid standard, it is so easy to give. Try it. Decide to say at least two things positive to your child each day. Make sure they are appropriate. Once you decide on two, you'll discover you have to give more. Your two will be "spent" before breakfast is finished.

So, let's agree: Parents ought be honest, open, and properly supportive of their children while resisting lies, deceits, and other cover-ups. Work at teaching your children how to face the natural consequences that abound from cradle to grave. You are in such a strategic position to do so.

To help you in your teaching task let's take a little walk down memory lane. The next chapter is a kind of Triptik of those incredible dazzling, dizzying, and dazing years from your own growing. To get in the proper frame of mind, lean back in your chair, close your eyes, and recall your first day in school. Remember what you wore? Remember how you felt? Remember the name of your first out-of-the-home teacher? Remember? And what else do you remember? Do you remember that it all happened in stages?

Good Old Golden-Rule Days

Down the dazzling road danced Dorothy and Scarecrow and Lion and Tin Man and Toto. Each step was progress of sorts. At least it was movement. If only she knew where she was, or where she was going, or how she would finally deal with the Wizard. But, never mind. They were on their way and the glistening yellow brick road stretched out before them.

Just in case it has slipped from your memory, I am remembering "The Wizard of Oz." In the off chance that you're unfamiliar with the story, you really ought to put reading it (or renting the movie) on your priority list. You will not only discover one of the great stories of our time, you'll also reexperience your school days' daze and be reminded of what your children are facing.

Everyone's school days are spent on that yellow brick road—a *changing* yellow brick road—going from where they are to somewhere else. Maybe Oz? The trip isn't bad. We can even dance down certain segments of that bright road so filled with the promise of excitement. It's marked with signs of progress as well. We always know when progress is upon us. We take a step—we graduate, a term derived from *gradus*, the Latin word for step. Taking a step is progress. It can even be a surprise. Maybe even fun. Was it for you?

One surprise most discover about the yellow brick road of school years is that it is longer than we had thought. To the child the road seems to have no end. It just keeps uncoiling, tantalizing them with the prospect that maybe—just maybe—this day will bring the end, the last of progress, steps, and unsettling change. Fat chance! The truth is that road has no end. It keeps on unwinding until, one day, you find the golden road takes you to the very different world of the teens. And still it doesn't stop, pressing on to the horizon of college, early twenties, marriage, family. Sometimes it finally dawns on even the dullest of us that the yellow brick road is not for getting somewhere. It's for traveling.

A second surprise is that the road, the scenery, and the ease or difficulty of travel all vary, depending on the day. Even depending on the person.

I'll never forget the father of a difficult daughter who strode into my office, slammed his gloves on the desk, and said, "Just when I think I'm finally understanding my daughter she changes. Again!" His daughter was not intentionally trying to be difficult. She was just nine going on 19. And she was skipping down the yellow brick road of her life, no more certain of what lay ahead than Dorothy—or her dad at her age. One thing is for certain about the yellow brick road and school days: Tomorrow the scenery will be different, and maybe even better.

A third surprise is that there's no way to stop on that road. I mean no stopping-stopping. There will be times when things move faster than at other times and may even appear to be at a standstill. But look around. Set your eyes on something that is truly permanent. You'll first sense and then see movement. That means some changes en route are more dramatic than others. And, yes, some are more complex than preceding ones. But at no point does the movement grind to a halt. It keeps moving, even stumbling on, sometimes faster, sometimes slower, sometimes hesitating before picking up the pace. But under all normal circumstances it does not stop.

To give you a feel for where you were, and give you some hint about where you child is, I'm going to sketch some road maps of sorts. Actually there will be four different "Triptiks" of the road most kids walk during the school years. One will be an overview of what is likely to happen to and in a child each year. That perspective will provide data to interpret the flow of events in your child's life, remind you of where you once walked, and offer some guesses about the next turns of the road.

A second Triptik will outline progress, school grade by school grade, with some information about what's happening in each. I must caution you that this is a compilation. Your child may be a little further ahead—or behind—the averages I will offer. There is an acceptable variation. Be conscious of it. All children don't move at the same speed. Effective parents must be like 16th-century navigators who used the stars, their sensing of the ocean's currents, some basic navigational tools, an eye out for certain birds and fish, and a few crude charts to make it from tiny port to tiny port. They didn't have all the help they would have liked, but enough to get the job done. Your feel for your child is crucial to how useful the second set of maps will be.

A third road map will offer a satellite view, great on expanse but weak on detail. Enough said.

But one of the most helpful maps to parents is a fourth. It's so useful I will start with it: the delightful story of Jesus and His parents near the end of what might be called His school daze. The account of what happened is in Luke

44

2:41–52, the only narrative in the Bible telling anything Jesus said or did between His birth and the beginning of His public ministry at age 30 or so. But this event speaks right to the heart of life in the elementary school years. Here's what Luke reports:

> *Every year His parents went to Jerusalem for the Feast of the Passover. When He was twelve years old, they went up to the Feast, according to the custom. After the Feast was over, while His parents were returning home, the boy Jesus stayed behind in Jerusalem, but they were unaware of it. Thinking He was in their company, they traveled on for a day. Then they began looking for Him among their relatives and friends. When they did not find Him, they went back to Jerusalem to look for Him. After three days they found Him in the temple courts, sitting among the teachers, listening to them and asking them questions. Everyone who heard Him was amazed at His understanding and His answers. When His parents saw Him, they were astonished. His mother said to Him, "Son, why have you treated us like this? Your father and I have been anxiously searching for you."*

"Why were you searching for Me?" He asked. "Didn't you know I had to be in My Father's house?" But they did not understand what He was saying to them.

Then He went down to Nazareth with them and was obedient to them. But His mother treasured all these things in her heart. (Luke 2:41–51)

Eleven verses. At first glance not much. But they teach so many important things about growing up, not the least of which is that Jesus, like your children, underwent the growing-up experience. Our Savior knows our circumstance. If there was nothing more, that would be a lot.

What made it easier for Him as He walked our road was that He had good models: Mary and Joseph. How do we know they were good models? It's right there in Luke's report: They took Him *with* them to the synagogue. That one action not only demonstrated better behavior, but showed us how family tradition is built through shared experience. Those are important insights to all travelers on the yellow brick road.

But all was not rosy in Jerusalem that morning. A terrible mix-up was brewing. Neither Mary nor Joseph nor Jesus wanted that experience. As with modern families, things just happen. It wasn't average, run-of-the-mill mis-communication: Mary and Joseph experienced what must have been three days of pure terror.

That's not the end of the story. Like most things that frighten families, the worst never happened. Jesus was found. Safe. There was an emotional reunion, slightly marred by Mary's outburst of understandable anxiety and confusion: "Son, why have you treated us like this? Your father and I have been anxiously searching for you" (Luke 2:48). His answer? A child's incomprehensible answer, confusing to the ears of a parent. It made little real sense to His mom or His dad. Truthful? Yes. Insightful? Yes! Unsettling? Yes! Mary didn't understand it. Still the exchange allowed for a peace pact, built on the principle of obedience—Jesus' obedience. Sensible kids know that doing what you are told keeps the parental temperature in the cool to moderate range.

They went home as they came: together, where a process long since begun in the lives of all three, continued. Using Luke's language, Jesus "grew." That doesn't mean He got bigger. No, the fullest meaning of Luke's word is something like "struggled on" or "hacked forward" or "beat into shape." All those perfectly good translations imply significant effort and struggles, and call for concentrated energy.

The areas in which Jesus grew? Four. He struggled on (1) intellectually, (2) physically, (3) spiritually, and (4) socially, just like you and I, no matter our age, *are doing right now*. Sound normal? From the infant years until we die, we tussle and turn, wrench and twist, push and press in those four areas. All four. If we do it well, we develop in a fifth way too. We grow emotionally, for emotional stability is nothing but the successful linkage and coming together of our intellectual, physical, spiritual, and social self. Think about it for yourself. Think about it for your child.

So, check out this "map" again and again. The specifics will vary over time as does the intensity of every foot of Jesus' well-rutted road. Everyone makes the trip. The greater our sense of awareness while doing so, the speedier and safer we make it to the goal of maturity. So much for Triptik 4—a great one.

Triptik 3 is more like an overview as seen from satellite. It gives the widest view of childhood, great in scope but weak on detail. Yet, it has value. It is sketched for us by developmental generalists who divide the school years into three large segments.

The first segment covers the period from the last months of about age 3 to the end of age 5—years in which boys and girls discard the last remaining vestiges of babyhood and become full-blown, curiosity-driven, genuine children. The days of baby talk over, the children push hard into new worlds, doing it so fast it scares you. Sometimes when they shove, they make big, loud mistakes. But the scale of our overview is so large that a big mistake at five is hardly a blip on anyone's experiential Richter scale.

The second segment scans from age 6 (or first grade) to 10 or 11. This segment is tougher to map because so many physical and social realities crowd in on it. They are absorbed at such different rates from child to child. In this changing scene, it is a not-fully-understood fact that girls today are beginning menstruation as much as 18 months earlier than just a generation ago. Not all—just many. It appears that the terminus of childhood and the onset of adolescence are sliding on the time line toward each other. Nevertheless, the chunk of childhood time is a kind of unit all by itself. Kids know that. Watch them at play. They show that they know.

That leads to the third and last segment of the satellite overview, the one that picks up at the far edge of about 11 years of age and lasts to about 14. To a large extent this third segment edges into the earliest of three later teen phases. That makes the preadolescent years hard to encapsulate. We will share much about them, and the wonder of the teen years, in the sequel to this book, which focuses on effective parenting of teens.

So there you have Triptik 3. Take the time to spot your child on the landscape. Be sure you don't put children where you wish they were or think they ought to be. Note where they are. That's all.

The next two maps are more detailed. One is based on a well-traveled summary by Dr. Gordon Bishop, an educator, former principal, school superintendent, and professor. His description of life in the grades will not fit every school but, in general, he offers a synopsis of what is happening inside the classrooms, grade by grade. Fleshing out his scenario are comments of many practicing preschool, kindergarten, and elementary schoolteachers.

1. In kindergarten (age 5 or so), the child works at developing social skills, works at understanding the purpose and value of rules, practices the things that make for readiness. It's an exploratory time. There's no advantage to doing kindergarten "better." But a child can indicate he or she is not ready to move on.

2. Grade 1 is a switch from kindergarten's guided play to Academics 101. Seat work enters their lives. Extended school hours reorganize their days. Early vestiges of self-discipline are required. The big discov-

ery for most—reading. New stuff every day. It may not be new to you, but it's surely new to them. Smart parents know this and focus on it. This is a great year for conversation. It'll happen if you let it.

3. Grade 2 is a breather year, the time of review for some and of catch-up for others. Second graders are old hands at school and at establishing friendships. They are fun to be around: cool, laid back, in control. But something is coming.

4. Grade 3 is another challenge year. Cursive writing needs mastering. Teacher expectations rise. Some schools require homework. For some kids the fun of learning begins to disappear. What a grand time for parents to move in with supportive conversation and discussion!

5. Being in the fourth grade means you have better muscle coordination. Writing, the physical art, is easier. Most make progress in sports and improve in other physical activities such as playing musical instruments. Many are now really ready for piano, guitar, and a fling at other fingered instruments—not all, but many.

6. Grade 5 is another of the easier years in which the children integrate previously learned skills and develop them to new highs. In many ways it's the late autumn of childhood.

7. Grade 6 is a toughie. For most it marks the onset of puberty, with erratic growth patterns—including spurts—and overall anxiousness. In some communities the youngsters are concerned about junior high *next* year. In others they wrestle with starting middle school *this* year. Materialism really rears its head with a desire to copy peers. And that costs money.

8. Students in grade 7 have usually become teenagers—but not all. Teen, or not, grade 7 is an up-and-down year with all four elements of Jesus' struggle (intellectual, physical, spiritual, and social) in wild interplay. The yellow brick road becomes a roller coaster during the teens. If you think that metaphor is clumsy, try remembering what it was like being 13. Like a Walt Disney cartoon flips from one wild thing to another, so go the days of the seventh grader. Life imitates art—or, does art imitate life?

With the breakthrough into the teens, Triptik 2 ends. What's coming? The wonder years of teendom, among the best life offers. But traveling in that world calls for another discussion, another day.

There is one more map that can help you help your children skip down their yellow brick roads. Triptik 1 traces the way based on years rather than grades. It's quite detailed and easily relates to the map of Luke, fleshing out what it means to grow, "in wisdom and stature and in favor with God and man." It's much more specific than that three-segment, satellite view. Year by year, through the elementary school period, your child deals with the concerns cited. And remember: not every child deals with every issue at the same time. Allow for normal variation. For sure, every child deals with all these things at *some* time.

- **Age 5:** Motor skills are developing, unevenly, not only between large muscles and small, but within categories. They perform some life tasks well and others poorly. Boys lag behind girls in coordination and physical development. They can be self-critical, able to carry out some responsibilities, interested in group activities. They can also be noisy, love vigorous exercise, and—oh, yes—they ask lots of questions. Parents should encourage them to do things for themselves and lead them to activities to help them experience the give and take of sharing. Try miniature golf with a five-year-old. In one hour you'll live out this entire paragraph.

- **Age 6:** Time for permanent teeth and the tooth fairy. Six-year-olds like being first and can be less cooperative than at five. They get into competition and do a lot of boasting. They can be less mature at home than outside. And they are active—better make that active, active, active. They have short attention spans but, as they learn to read, it expands. Reading is also their doorway to seeing a relationship between ideas.

- **Age 7:** All the physical aspects are in motion: Growth is steady, coordination is improving, vigorous and full-bodied activity is enjoyed. And, surprise, they are sensitive to the feelings of others and yearn for adult approval. What a time for parental affirmation! They begin to understand abstract concepts like time and money. They recognize that boys and girls are different and act differently. They can be competitive and quarrelsome. They have a concern for right and wrong, but they also have a tendency to steal small things. I once took a group of children through an exercise to identify how much something must be worth before you would call taking it "stealing." They made a nice discrimination: in general stealing began, for them, at taking things that cost 49 cents or more—except that taking *anything* from them was stealing.

- **Age 8:** Try integrating this: Eight-year-olds are alert, friendly, interested in people, careless, noisy, and argumentative. Best friends have become those of the same sex. Lots of boy-girl competition. Gangs (not the street variety but the clubhouse kind) begin to develop with the beginning of more allegiance to peers than adults (sometimes even Mom or Dad). They collect anything and everything. They need frequent reminding. They engage in more team games, by choice, and also develop a love for comics and adventure stories. They self-evaluate. They have more enthusiasm than judgment. The result of that collage of characteristics: Broken stuff—bikes, bottles, chairs, arms. They need a pal. It might be you.

- **Age 9:** Niners can be dependable, reasonable, and responsible, but also tend to get discouraged, especially under pressure. Girls are usually larger than boys. Both like rough and active games and get into arguments about fairness. They can make plans and can progress on their own. Individual skills and abilities become apparent. Gangs are strongest at this age.

- From here on, even this map gets murky because there are so many variables. But within age 10 and age 11 and up to the edges of age 12 (a time sometimes described as preadolescence), many things are happening. Secondary sex characteristics begin to develop. In these years kids can demonstrate an enormous appetite, but for a limited number of things. And even among those their yens are irregular. This is usually a period of rapid growth, with girls coming to maturity as much as two years before boys. "Awkward," "lazy," "restless," "rebellious," "over-critical," and "uncooperative" are words teachers and parents use to describe children during this time. Their maturity level varies remarkably. They become interested in earning money. They seek a sense of belonging and acceptance from peers and adults, hoping for warm affection, especially from adults. (Better underline that sentence!) It's the doorway to some wonderful—or some terrible—childhood experiences. Girls begin to demit from gangs but boys don't.

All of the four "maps" offered are incomplete. They lack the personalization of your son or daughter. And of you. These Triptiks are not a narrow groove in which every child fits, but a broad reminder of how much is happening in those few short years. I hope it also helps you see how broad the range is so that you and your child can relax a little. Let this chapter be a refamiliarization for you.

The point of this chapter? It's a refresher, a trip to your own roots. No matter what you think you did as a kid, this is the same yellow brick road you walked or stumbled or ran. Walking with your child is *déjà vu*, a reliving of your yesterday. The reason it seems different to you is that when you walked that way you had no yardstick to measure experience. Things just happened. As an adult you now see the experiences through eyes that measure, evaluate, rank, and qualify.

More than that, in your own instance you have leeched out a lot of the drama in these years because you know how the story ends—

at least your story. You grew up. Now, in your adult and parenting person, you are on another road. You are on the road of your late 20s, 30s, 40s, observing the progress of your child *while you, yourself, are trying to figure out the next moves in your life*. The parental life is not a monorail—it's at least double railed, maybe more, depending on how many people's needs demand your attention. And that's where we are going next.

In the next chapter the focus is clearly on you. We will focus on you because if you don't understand your present stroll in life, you'll never understand the pell-mell dash of your elementary school child or the later tumbling intensity of the teens. Compared to them, your world may seem serene. But there are deep and strong currents that are just as insistent on carrying you along as other rip-roaring events sweep along your child. The big word, maybe the biggest? Change.

You and Your Shadows— and Change

How about a trivia question? Try this one: "What singer made the song 'Me and My Shadow' famous?" Give up? Ted Lewis.

I suppose the next question for many will be, "Who's Ted Lewis?" For the benefit of baby boomers and their successors he was a some-time singer and big-band leader in the 1930s and 1940s, occasionally featured in films. "Me and My Shadow" was his theme song. He would present it wearing a battered top hat, carrying a cane, and doing a little soft-shoe dance while a spotlight created that shadow. That song popped into my mind as I searched for a title to visualize this chapter. Bang, there it was— Ted Lewis' song! I added an important "s," shifted pronouns, and added a word. In so doing, the caption portrayed the three accents of this chapter: (1) you, (2) shadowy presences, and (3) change.

Do I need to repeat for whom this book is prepared? Sure I do. Repetition is the mother of learning, or so said the Romans. It's prepared for you, the parent, the first and most important accent of the three. The only reason we presented the last chapter was to give an overview of what's happening in the life of your elementary school child so that *you* can be a more effective parent. And each succeeding chapter of this book is prepared to help you stay in the effective parenting groove. No question about it: You are the subject of *School Daze*. As such it is very important that you have a good picture of yourself. If you don't want to know about yourself, or don't think that a better understanding of who you are has anything to do with effective parenting, you better start flipping pages. Quick. But if you want to understand the messages of other effective parents and of the elementary schoolteachers, proceed in a deliberate and thoughtful way. In doing so let's turn to those shadows that follow you everywhere.

Shadowlike presences, never fully disconnected, trail every parent. Here's where the metaphor stumbles. Sometimes the shadow is ours. Sometimes it's someone else's. How many presences? Three or four, for sure—maybe five or ten! It's important that we acknowledge their presence and recognize their power.

Let me give an example of a shadowy presence of someone else: The shadowy presence of your son or daughter no matter where you or they are. Once you have a child, the way you think about everything changes. Right? As infants they affect where you can go, and when, and how long you can stay. Actually, *they* don't do that. Your sense of responsibility for them does that. But *they* trigger that sense of responsibility. As time goes by, your sense of your children's needs and wants influences where the family vacations, your choices of jobs, maybe even your work habits. Even older, well into college and beyond, they still influence your schedule and permeate your thoughts. Finally, when they are fully grown and gone (you think!), you discover they aren't gone at all. They keep on affecting you. Grandparents choose a retirement location, "because of our children"—whether it's to stay near them or get as far away as possible. The shadow of the child exerts power for as long as you live.

Isaiah quotes God as asking, "Can a mother forget the baby at her breast?" (Is. 49:15). Of course not. But then a mom or dad can't forget their grown child either. Once you bring a child into the world, a bond is established that never shatters. Until we die, we are never more than a thought away from our son or daughter. They overshadow us.

Ditto spouses. More shadows. Husbands and wives who are serious about their marriage vows are intertwined for life. What better understanding of Adam's words that Eve is now "bone of my bones and flesh of my flesh" (Gen. 2:23) than the metaphor of shadow and shadowed? To indicate how serious this connection is, there are studies that show that husbands and wives, over time, mirror each other in speech, thought, and attitude. Some claim spousal appearances, especially their facial expressions, combine, and that those who make a vow of faithfulness for "as long as we both shall live" begin to look like each other. Is that possible?

The two examples of extrapersonal shadows are not the whole of it. There are more: friends, ideals, philosophies. They layer their attitudes and goals on ours to the point that they may look like one and the same. But there are other shadows casting their influence upon us. Shadows like our yesterdays. No one escapes the shadowed reality of our past.

Effective parents had a lot to say about the influence of the past in *Then Comes the Baby in the Baby Carriage*. Remember? They didn't equivocate. They plainly stated that much of what they do now, and how they think, is a gift (or burden) from yesterday, passed to them through their parents, grandparents, even great-grandparents. The way many families fix their Thanksgiving turkey dressing (you put *what* in the stuffing?) reflects how the wife's or husband's mom or grandmother made it.

Whether Christmas presents are opened on Christmas Day or Christmas Eve likely imitates what at least one marriage partner did as a child. Even the bedtime prayers you use are usually the prayers a grandmother first learned and then passed down to you through the generations. Lots of little chunks of yesterday cast their shadows over you.

But the most intense shadow trailing your life is none of those three. The sharpest shadows cast by us or over us are those of what we used to be and how we used to think or act. No one fully discards a yesterday, as if it were a snakeskin to be shed and left behind. The most we can do is layer coats of newness over our past, covering it as best we can (or think we must). It's not gone, only veiled.

In the meanwhile the process continues. What Luke tells us in chapter 2, verse 52 about increasing and struggling forward is a lifelong procedure. Even as we wrestle with all that our yesterday means, we are moving out into a not fully known or understood tomorrow. We are changing; we are changing every day. Often it's only the shadows of yesterday that keep us from forgetting all that we once were. A parent who forgets she or he was once a child and is moving toward being a grandparent someday is not going to be a very effective parent.

It's hard for some to accept that our life development is never complete. They don't want to think about a daily transitioning to something they are not yet (and a changed "something" at that). They don't think much, or at all, of Luke's four areas of tussling: the intellectual, the physical, the spiritual, and the social. Like Popeye the sailor some would rather say, "I am what I am, and that's all that I am." But they aren't.

Let's pause here a moment and think again of the accents in this chapter. You? Yes. Shadows? Yes. And what else? Change. In the parenting process we must always remember our own past and the changes that have taken place through it and because of it. Life is progressive. The Peter Pan approach of "I don't want to grow up!" is not a choice. A growth process is automatic, built into our being. The Greek term that Luke uses to describe the way Jesus moved through the four areas of development can be translated as "hacking or struggling forward." Life is a struggle. In healthy people it always has a forward movement. It means change. And, would you believe it, it is predictable.

With some variation vigorous shifting happens to grade schoolers each year of their life. That's what we talked about in the last chapter. And significant ups and downs strike teens in three- or four-year cycles. These same cycles continue through adulthood and on into old age—only they are best seen when measured with decades. While we are rearing our changing children, we are facing a menu of significant changes in our own lives. Think of it: Our children are moving, each in their own orbits of change at speeds related to their age, and parents are doing the same thing, at speeds related to their age. No wonder there's turmoil in family life! Everyone is in motion. Nobody stands still. We all keep moving forward while trailing the shadowy presences of our yesterdays.

We can and ought to get specific. Let's review the parental changes that so affect the way we deal with our children. I can walk you through what normally happens to parent-persons during their 20s, their 30s, their 40s, and their 50s. I'll highlight the decadal happenings against Luke's four areas: the intellectual, the physical, the spiritual, and the social. Much more happens beyond your 50s but not many at those ages are parenting elementary school children. Spot yourself in our march across the years. And pay attention to your spouse's time line. As much as you need to understand your children, you need to understand your partner as well. Same rules: The descriptives are broad and may not fit you precisely in this moment of your life. But, believe me, they will fit. Let's start with the 20s.

- **The 20s:** Somewhere in their 20s most who become parents have their first child. Not all—just most. Some may even have their second. What an interesting time of life to embark on founding a family! A husband and wife in their 20s have probably finished their formal education in this decade. They are taking a first whack at applying abstract ideas and ideals to life. The 20s are days of gusto, a little low on detached, intellectual reflection. There's not a lot of yearning for intellectual stimulation. Most have just escaped the years of training and aren't eager for more.

The physical? The 20s are peak years of health and vitality in which the gusto approach can cause problems, especially in a couple's sex life. Over the long pull a healthy sex life needs more than unbridled vigor. It needs healthy portions of tenderness, caring, and understanding. And like everything else physical, it requires monitoring and adjusting. Oh, yes, one thing more: in the 20s, physical growth finally stops. Finally.

Look around a church. You don't have to be a Sherlock Holmes to realize that the 20s are tough spiritual days. No wonder. Much of the time the gusto life is in conflict with the values learned in an earlier time. Add this age's normal cynicism toward institutional anything, church included, and you have trouble. But (and this is a wonderful but) there is hope.

Deep within the 20-year-olds, core values and beliefs still exist and churn. If either partner follows the Spirit's leading to live the Christ-life more fully, the other will often follow.

In terms of things social a lot is happening. The young mom and dad are not yet fully released from their past and so have not yet developed clear social identity. That takes time. To achieve this identity those in their 20s make serious efforts to separate from their families of origin to stake out new worlds of identity. What usually keeps the young couple linked to Mom and Dad is the materialism their parents sowed in their lives. I mean, how many parents encourage their kids toward education, arguing that college is the way to the fullest life in Christ? Some, but the larger number attend college because parents tell them education is the doorway to jobs, money, and success. More. When the kids are in their 20s, those same moms and dads become the source for wedding receptions, down payments for homes, job references, and co-signers for loans. No surprise that sons and daughters want to be on their own and achieve a little breathing room. How better to do this than to set some goals of their own, hum a tune to their liking, and carve their own Thanksgiving turkeys—with their own new friends?

- **The 30s:** In the 30s the intellectual fervor changes. The 30s are the season of educational seminars and practical-functional development. This decade surfaces a great concern for all the things they weren't taught in their earlier formal education. These are days dedicated to self-improvement, often too dedicated. Toward the end of this decade some signs of passage appear every bit as wondrous as the movement from early teens (13–15) to middle teens (16–18) when the question shifted from "What's going to happen?" to "What's happening?" For most, the 30s' life doesn't have a very wide-angle lens. But it will. In the 40s.

During the 30s, energetic, child-raising years, physical limits begin to appear for the athletic or the very active. They are not as young as they once were. Theirs is the age when professional athletes talk of retirement. At home two interesting "physical" things happen to couples in their 30s: The male sex drive wanes a bit while the female's increases. Since they weren't equal to begin with, this is no big deal, but it does signal future changes in sexual relations and the need to talk. A couple's sex life can be very central in the 30s if it is tended by both.

Spirituality deepens for many in the 30s. Their parentally-sown materialism still looks pretty good, but its raw edges are starting to show. There's an openness, even a hunger, for a spirituality that will flesh out the faith of their formative years. The 30s are a field of great opportunity for churches that are attuned to the needs and questions of these revitalizable seekers.

Socially the 30s are the years of civic consciousness. Many join civic clubs and get active in politics at this age. It's also the time the family environment is intentionally developed apart from the job. Work and home are not two elements of the same reality. They are clearly seen as different and are separated. In summary there's not much socializing that isn't related to the three worlds of the 30s: home, community, and work. Why? Time.

- **The 40s:** The 40s, too, are fascinating. This is the decade of intellectual, physical, spiritual, and social change. With a vengeance.

The intellectual energies are focused on knowledge required for a career change or toward retraining in the old career. Who/what caused this back-to-school movement? A number of things: (1) Some see that their vocational field has moved ahead in the years since they entered it, and they sense that there are changes that have gotten away from them. (2) There are all those younger women and men who are charging into the field as competition with different, and often better, training. (3) It's also very likely that by 40 a person has changed jobs and additional knowledge is required to make the change a success. (4) Some discover that in their second round of training, they enjoy the educational experience more than they had thought and are better at it than they had imagined.

Physical changes that began in the 30s continue into the 40s. Limits of strength appear. One or more of your children may be teens and looking like a competitor. Some fathers, especially fathers, have a tendency to distance themselves from their teen children because they haven't yet worked out how to relate to children who are now physically and intellectually on a par.

Those changes set the stage for intriguing spiritual changes too. As our 40-year-old reviews past intellectual and physical decisions, with lots of "why-did-I's" imbedded into them, guilt over past mistakes rears its head. A few of those in their 40s toughen their stance toward God and religion, casting much blame on either. Yet others return to the church, seeing it with new appreciation for past religious teachings and experiences. This is a great time to find a church that is supportive, for support is desperately needed.

These are social years as both husband and wife have fewer responsibilities for their growing children. For the first time, many come face-to-face with their aging as their own parents become ill and many die. Vocational limits appear and most adults by now develop a sense of how far they will advance at work. This affects how they relate to others, for these are years when many adults avoid, and are jealous of, those who have gone further in the world.

The decade of the 40s is a demarcation between great eras. What's coming is not better than what has gone before. Nor is it worse. It's just markedly different.

- **The 50s:** This is a truly new and different land, the 50s. In the years 1940 to 1970, living into the fifth decade meant for almost everyone that your children were out of elementary school. Not so today. Today there are many who chose to have children later in life. For them the 50s is still a time for attending PTA and dealing with preadolescents that must be faced from a perspective not experienced before, for the 50s are full of intellectual excitement. Some are getting additional training for a last big vocational step. Their intellectual abilities remain strong for now they know that old dogs learn tricks easier and faster than new dogs—but they like to deny that is true. Experience proves to be such an asset for those in their 50s! It largely neutralizes the advantages of those who are younger with better educations.

But there is an oops! We are forced to recognize that almost everything physical (hearing, sight, sense of touch, and so much else) declines at the rate of about one percent per year and has been since the mid 40s. This may be the decade in which we face our first health crisis. Physical limits are not clear and limitations may not be denied.

In matters spiritual the 50s are the age of individualism in which we are freed from quasi-theological commitments to the past. That means people in their 50s differentiate between what God clearly wants of and for them from much of the cultural baggage that they had substituted for religion. They look for meaning in their lives and have hope of discovering it because they have learned how to be critical of themselves, others, and society without giving up on any.

Our social self gets a bump. This is the decade when the nest empties. Even if we begin it with an elementary school student in our home, he/she likely leaves during this decade. And how do we compensate? We turn to our families of origin—to brothers and sisters. Cousins, too. The 50s is the decade we attend reunions and reclaim old friends. It is also the period when many decide they need newer and younger friends.

To complete this complex picture of what happens between 21 and 59 I must add one more important element. Not only are we changing as individuals, but the world around us is changing as well. By decades. Historians and social commentators name the 30s, the 40s, the 50s, the 60s, the 70s, the 80s, and the 90s. Each is tagged as a distinctive period. We live our lives within the broader report of history.

So what might help us keep our heads during these very different times? One is someone who loves our children as much as we do—or almost so. Who wants the same "best" that any parent wants. Your children's teachers. The next chapter gives them a chance to speak to the themes we have spotted and in a way that each of us can face our "you," be comfortable with the shadowy presences, and develop the skills to profit from inescapable change.

Teachers Talk—A Few Kids Too

---◆---

Who speaks for families? Observer voices? The voices of "specialists" pressing this new theory of family systems or that fascinating conjecture about rearing children? Usually. Sad to say, little has been heard from those for whom parenting is much more than a matter for scholarly investigation. But that's not the case in this series. Parental voices dominated in *Then Comes the Baby in the Baby Carriage*. That's partly true with this book too. They are the primary contributors to some chapters and a distinct presence in others.

The outgrowth of effective parenting, the sons and daughters of those great moms and dads, get their moments too. Their remarks pepper each book of this series, including a collage of compelling comments from elementary-grade-school sons and daughters who are part of this chapter.

That leaves one remaining party to the world of effective parenting of *grade-school* kids. Teachers.

Teachers? Yes, teachers. Who has a better seat for all that happens in their students' homes? Every day—before, during, and after all home crises—teachers are drawn into an active part in their students' lives. We had an indication of their perspective in chapter 1. Remember how easily they fingered the importance of letting elementary school children face the natural consequences of their actions? That insight poured in as one voice from teachers at all the grade levels, from every corner of the U.S.A. The family's or teacher's country of origin, race, economic circumstance, or family composition made no difference. It is fascinating that few teachers knew how strongly most other teachers felt about it. Why? *Nobody had asked them*. But we did.

When I wrote *Then Comes the Baby in the Baby Carriage*, I sought insights from effective parents. I asked pastor friends to nominate effective parents. My co-workers came through. Based on their recommendations I wrote the parents, asking for their views on effectiveness and how it is achieved. The random method of their selection and the number who responded gave statistical credibility to their responses. I am confident that I reported accurately what

Christian parents, in all of life's circumstances, feel contributes to effectiveness.

In the preparation of this book about effectively parenting grade-school-age children, I did much the same thing. Only instead of probing only parents I also turned to teachers, grades K–6, for insight, advice, and comment. In some instances I asked entire faculties, in both public schools or Christian schools, to share things they thought parents of their students should know and practice. Did they respond? Did they ever! And it didn't take me long to find threads of commonality, the thickest one reported in chapter 1!

While gathering material from classroom teachers, I also happened to speak at a number of teacher's conferences. I couldn't resist asking their opinions to test the responses I was receiving from other teachers. No matter how I couched questions about what parents ought to do for their elementary school children, the same kinds of answers poured forth. I turned the teacher's comments into declaratory sentences and took them to other conferences, seeking reaction or validation. The teachers agreed with their peers from other places. This process developed a lot of data—and data about data. In short I learned a lot.

I spotted their high degree of agreement and the narrow span of the teachers' comments. While effective parents had a high degree of agreement on many things, there was also a lot of left-over comments—specific items that one or two parents animatedly supported which the rest largely ignored. Not so with teachers. Elementary teachers had a half dozen things they absolutely pounded into the ground, and very little else to say. I wondered why.

My guess is that elementary schoolteachers mostly present basic courses—fundamentals. There are few frills in the grade-school curriculum. Elementary schoolteachers just naturally nail down the fundamentals of parenting at the elementary-school level and leave it at that. That's my guess.

This chapter contains two new categories of these basic teacher concerns. The last chapters will isolate five more teacher emphases, for a total of eight. Add the concerns of parents from *Then Comes the Baby in the Baby Carriage* and we'll have more than 20 different grass-roots items that contribute to effective parenting. We total them like that because the suggestions in this book build on the accents of the previous one.

Twenty. That's not a lot to keep in mind—about the same number of things you must remember to execute a golf swing, operate a power saw, or use a computer.

To better understand the suggestions of parents and teachers I also talked to a number of seventh- and eighth-graders. I asked them to comment about the parenting they have experienced. They didn't make any statements. They couched their comments in the safer form of questions. The 10 questions I isolated for this chapter recurred in almost identical language no matter where in the U.S.A. I interviewed. I talked with seventh- and eighth-graders because they are the most recent graduates of elementary school *and* the elementary-school family. I accept their comments as descriptive of real, grade school family life. But they do not suggest ways to improve the situation. "Why not," I asked? "When we comment no one listens," say they. Ouch! Whether that's true is not important for now. It's their view. I accept their questions as validation of the accuracy of what teachers say—*and* as revealing commentary of effective parenting areas that need attention and help.

Ready or not, let's hear it from the kids, unedited and to the point.

- Why do parents always think they are right?

- Why do parents claim to listen to your side of a story, but don't?

- Why do parents always lecture and preach rather than make their point and be done with it?

- Why do parents tell you not to do things they do themselves?

- Why do parents say they trust us but won't let us do so many things?

- When parents tell a story, why do they change it to make us look stupid?

- How do parents know the right age to do something? Why don't parents understand?

- Why do our parents treat me and my sister/brother so differently?

- Why do parents become angry and yell at us for no reason?

If you feel those 10 questions don't fit your family, I won't argue. You may be right. But I've never placed that list before elementary school children without their exuberant affirmation. And, yes, I do realize these are questions that *children* shaped from their perspective. But the concession is not the point. The point is that children ask those questions based on their perception of reality. What is sad and somewhat disheartening about them is not that they are asked, but that many adults say they have never "heard" these questions before.

So, when a child whines out question 9, a "don't be silly we treat you all alike" isn't a very useful answer. Nor will that response end the matter. Give them an honest answer. Tell them that no two children are ever treated alike because they are not alike. Even if you could prove you have spent exactly the same amount of time with each of them, that would not satisfy the complaint. The complaint has to do with feelings. Your child "feels" he or she is being treated unfairly. *That's* the point. You can't dispute feelings. They just are. A child's feelings are so real and have so much power in them. Left unattended into adulthood, these feelings become the pool out of which psychiatrists make their living and from which counselors lift their clients.

That's enough from the kids for the moment. This is not a book about elementary school *children*. It's a book about elementary school children's *parents*, especially those who are, or who want to be—effective. Mark the page with those preadolescent comments for review later.

We must move on to two new items of teacher talk. Both have to do with building partnerships.

One concerns itself with developing a partnership between you and your child. The other has to do with building a partnership with your child's teacher.

I do not bring these two up at this point because they are of second and third importance. They aren't. These just happen to be on my pile of matters of equal importance. And they are connected. The first: *Read to them.*

Read to them? I first assumed that an English teacher slipped in that comment about things parents could do to help their school-age kids deal with life.

But then came another: *Read, read, read to your children. Don't stop reading just because they are in school. So much is happening when you are reading to them.* Oops. That doesn't sound like an English teacher.

And yet another: *Read to your child and let him/her read to you. Even 12-year-olds like to share a good book.*

More comments poured in on the subject of reading with/to/for your children than any other—so many that I could not ignore the point. Many teachers view your reading aloud to children, or together with them, as an important part of parenting the elementary school child. But why?

My answer came from remembering. For eight years I was a kind of superintendent of education for a five-state school system. I don't know much about education systems, as such, so I did the next best thing. I visited every classroom at least once and watched tremendous teachers in action. What I learned by seeing!

I concluded that reading aloud is a teacher's secret weapon. When life in the classroom gets tough, or when teachers want a bit of a rest, they either read to the children or have the children read to each other. Both ways work. Once alerted to this dynamic, I found it at work everywhere. Reading aloud, or reading together, happens in all the best classrooms. Its considerable educational value notwithstanding, it fills time in an important, but amiable, way. When the kids read, the teacher blends into the chalkboard. They take over—children teaching one another—and liking it. Our "experts" are giving us solid guidance through their suggestion that parents read to and with their children.

But what if we substituted watching TV together? Won't that serve the same purpose? TV is a family bonding experience too. Right?

Not really. Watching TV together is not the same as reading together. Television offers little participation in the moment. How can you ask "What does that mean?" while the TV program, even an educational one, pounds on toward the conclusion with the intensity of a runaway train? Unless you have a VCR with a pause button, any attempt to explain will leave you in the program's dust. About the best you can hope for is a fortuitous commercial break. But reading! Reading is made for pauses and interjections and comments and diversions and sharing. Sharing, especially. That's a second benefit the teacher's admonition toward reading offers: It not only profitably fills time with educational potential, it builds relationships as well.

Remember reading to your littlest one? Remember how she sat on your lap and turned the pages? The bonding was so intense that your legs hurt! And the squirmy, listening child was not only busily developing small motor muscles by pushing and pawing through the book ("let *me* turn the pages"), making sure you didn't skip anything, but a feeling of wondrous closeness enveloped the two of you. Remember that? Let's hear it for reading!

And when your wee one grew a little older, remember how he snuggled up to you, or lay with his head in your lap as you read, his weight and warmth exuding a drowsy camaraderie? More relational memories. Educational, too. And that's the teacher's point. Don't stop educational/relational reading. There's no reason that kind of uplifting activity has to evaporate from the parenting scene. All it takes is a commitment on your part to wedge out the time. Your teacher friends are saying that reading to and with your child is worth the effort. Parental commitment to this joint activity will not only enhance their reading skill, their appreciation of literature, and their body of knowledge, but it will help keep you close.

Close. That's a second area of concern teachers want to develop with parents—so parents can be better parents and they can be better teachers. They want to be close to you. They want you to be close to them. *"Talk to me,"* they say.

I know, I know. Everyone has heard horror stories about bad things that happened because a parent was open with the child's teacher. Don't let a bad experience stop you. Best yet, don't believe them. Most never happened—really. Actually, I think most stories about parents and teachers in tension are exaggerated extensions of childhood apprehensions we had about teachers. Or maybe they are a little piece of guilt left over from when we tried to justify our efforts to neutralize some natural consequence in our child's life—and got caught. Maybe? No matter. Whatever is truth, decide to start anew. Decide to do three things teachers suggest for being a more effective parent:

- *Be informed. Meet the teacher. Attend orientation meetings. Read the letters from school. Go to parent/teacher conferences prepared with questions.*

  What better way to be informed about what is happening during the largest single segment of your child's waking hours? Talk with the teacher who is there. Claim the opportunities offered. Effective parents may not be perfect but they are always curious. Kids usually say their parents are nosey. Good! Parents ought to be, especially about-things they are invited to investigate. Ask teachers about things you do not understand. Seek advice. Work at developing a common strategy for dealing with difficulties your child may face or for helping your child claim the best from new opportunities. All it takes is Winston Churchill's call to "Talk, talk, talk."

- *Share information that will help the teacher understand the student (your child) better.*

  Decide to keep the teacher informed about unsettling things in your child's life. How? Send a note. If it's serious enough, make an appointment. The teacher is on your side. You are setting up a team-teaching opportunity in which both your child's teachers (you of the school-in-your-home and your partner from the elementary school) are fully informed.

- *Please don't criticize other parents, teachers, or students in front of your children.*

  Withhold judgement. Be fair. If something seems odd to you, or comes home twisted so badly that it doesn't make sense, go talk to the teacher. Offer that same opportunity to your child's teacher. Teachers care about your child and want the best for your loved one. Talk to the teacher *before* you reach a conclusion.

As one teacher wrote: *Please don't talk down the school in front of your child. Support us. If you aren't sure of something, come talk to us in private. We may not always agree, but we can always talk.*

If it seems to you that I have shifted the focus in this chapter away from you as the effective parent, I haven't. The reason we are concerned is that to a large degree your style of relating with the teacher bleeds over to other areas of your life. That elementary school-teacher is not the only one with whom you team teach. You have a spouse, right? All the dynamics of relationship cited above are at work in your marriage as well. Three ideals fit—whether the focus of your concern is your relationship to your child, your child's teacher, your child's other parent, or others: (1) Get the facts before you act; (2) share basic information with those who can help your child more if they know it; 3) don't shoot yourself in the foot by criticizing those whom your child sees as friend and helper. Effective parents maximize those relationships to help them become even more effective.

From time to time you may feel as if you are there to help the teacher do his or her work. Never. One great teacher put it this way: *Parents are the most important people in a child's life. Being a parent is a lifelong commitment but it is most intense during the first dozen or so years of a child's life. We educators are there to help the parents in their responsibility of rearing the child and preparing them for life.*

I like that. Not only is it true but it also lets us know how teachers feel about us parents and about their relationship to us. Throughout the rest of this book you'll receive other wonderful tips from teachers to help you strive to be an effective parent. Accept their help in the spirit it is offered. They are on your side.

Life in the Same Boat

As the first words of this chapter fall to paper I feel the presence of many effective parents who have given of themselves so that others might grow as moms and dads. One exciting thing is their belief that the skill is not reserved for only a few. They believe anyone can reach their level of parental effectiveness. As a matter of fact, they are surprised everyone isn't already doing what they do. None of them see their practice of parenting as unusual or impossible to copy. Maybe that's clue 1 to effective parents: They believe they do what any parent would do.

I started my study of effective parenting by following the directions of a 13th-century French recipe for rabbit stew: "First, catch the rabbit." I decided I had to isolate some effective parents for study purposes. That was easy. Reliable folks of all kinds can recognize, and will quickly identify, moms and dads who are doing a great job rearing their children. Please note this: While parenting seems to be a task for couples, there are many single parents who fit the effective parenting pattern. It's just harder for them.

I wrote hundreds of them, asking that they tell me how they do what they so effectively do. I received more than a thousand pages of their insights to which I added many hours of personal interviews. When I was done with the research, there lay out before me a baker's dozen characteristics which effective parents said were important.

Would those 13 characteristics be present in parents of elementary school children? No question. Effective parenting is effective parenting at every level of life. Only the specifics vary. And the ranking of importance may be reorganized from grade to grade. Here's the checklist:

- **Sense of Humor**—I haven't mentioned this first because it was ranked number 1 by parents. (Actually nothing was ranked number 1 by the group.) Humor is the characteristic of effective parents that caught me most by surprise and is the most difficult to define. As I read their comments about the importance of humor, I was puzzled by the limp illustrations they offered. I never developed a clear picture but I deduced a couple things.

First, in effective families it is *shared* humor. Sometimes all the family is present when the funny thing happens. Sometimes the humor is wrapped in some common experience which, whenever something like it happens again, causes all to laugh. Stories like that often begin, "It was like the time when we ...." And everyone gathers at the altar of some experience they understand and share.

Second, the subject of their laughter and hilarity isn't very amusing. Not to outsiders. Little of it would make anyone's joke book, which is another way of saying that family humor is more family than humor. Families, in laughter, are saying to each other, "I trust you." More times than not, the laughter revolves around an earthy or surprising turn of events featuring one member. Without the spirit of oneness and good will, the event often would only be embarrassing. So what tempers the embarrassment? The substance of the moment, making it pleasant and even acceptable, is that wondrous thing called love.

- **Love**—I will be puzzled to my dying day by families that don't daily say and do love at each other as they walk through life. I don't understand moms or dads who stumble over showing love or who hesitate using the word. Effective parents all agree with me. Oh, yes, they are offended by meaningless muttering of "I love you." Who isn't? But substituting silence for a sincere expression of affection is incomprehensible to them. Effective families say love. They *do* love. They wallow in love. They make sure that no one in their clan ever doubts the intensity of parental affection. They are determined to spread love through words, acts of kindness, and gifts.

- **Touch**—I've always been touchy about touch. Touching is such a personal thing and somehow unseemly as a public display. But, wait a minute! Look at all the TV touching that goes on. No, not the groping of R-rated movies. I mean in politics, in sports, in daily events. It's quite amazing, really. Touching is common at every level of life from the mayor's embrace, to the athletes' patting, to the handholding of a child. It's everywhere. And even a little biblical study will reveal how much touching took place in the life of Jesus.

When effective parents talk about touching, they put it right at the heart of their world. They hug. They hold-hands. They link arms. They brush against each other with casual ease as expression of their family unity. While touching does not necessarily make for effectiveness, effectiveness inevitably includes touching. One dad said, "When my father didn't touch me, I wasn't sure he loved me." Parents must take time to touch.

- **Time**—The effective parent hoots at any who glibly mouths that while they are unable to give quantity time to their family they gladly share quality time. Quality time! Effective families agree: There is no such thing as quality time that is not also quantity time. There is quantity time that has little quality to it—but not the inverse. One parent wrote, "Little children spell love, T-I-M-E."

And they back it with actions. Story after story poured out of effective parents about dropping other activities in order to have family time, changing jobs for family time, and planning vacations that would maximize family time. The examples were impressive. Their children's responding determination to do the same was impressive as well.

- **Roots**—Most effective parents give the credit for their attitudes to the homes where they were raised. They were honest about it: Some couples didn't have a good home in their growing years. They use their parent's model as the way to not relate to their children.

  We can't do much about our history. We cannot choose our ancestors. But effective families study them. They dig around in their families of origin, lifting out things of value that will strengthen them in their parenting days. They treasure the values that were ingrained in them by their parents and grandparents, values which now just naturally fall into place. That's how effective parents still honor their fathers and their mothers. They do things for their children that their parents did for them. And they do it with enthusiasm.

- **School-in-the-home**—Being effective parents is a role they consciously play. They see their home as an accredited school and themselves as the faculty. They do not teach by default. They see themselves as teaching by choice. That's one reason their attitude toward time is so intentional and is arrived at so easily. They need great gobs of time for their teaching task. Once they've isolated time, they know what to do with it. They teach. Every family moment—the sad ones and the glad ones—those tragic and those triumphant—are seen by effective parents as pregnant with educational possibilities. As long as the child is a child and in their home, the classes are in session.

One last thing: They do not educate by default—and it's not because the elementary school system, public or private, has failed them. Effective parents believe that much (most?) of their children's education is their specific responsibility, something that cannot be done by anyone else. *They* are the parents and, hence, the teachers in the home. They believe there are subjects which can only be taught in the home: things such as morality, values, family history, love, forgiveness, and sharing. No other school in the world can offer those courses to their children as effectively as they can. And no one else, anywhere, is as fully qualified to teach their children. They do not give up on those points.

- **Change**—Effective parents realize that teaching is tough. One reason is the ever-present struggle with change all teachers face. If only parents could pass on to their children the things they had received, teaching exactly as they had been taught. But the world has taken many a spin since these effective moms and dads walked in their children's oxfords. There *are* similarities between the subject matters of yesterday and those of today, but there are also—always—surprising twists that call for reinterpretation and adaptation. Change.

  Does that mean effective parents are willowy in their convictions or granite hard? Neither. They weigh the new moment and calculate the reason, and implication, of change. They don't start many sentences with, "We've always." Nor are they swayed by, or sympathetic to, a child's argument that starts, "Everyone else is." Somewhere in the world between those two poles, effective parents go about their business of measuring change, weighing it, giving it value, and deciding what to do. They don't go at change with blinders or hankering for approval from their children, no matter the price. They see their approach as duty and as joy, giving to their young what is exclusively parental property in the home: their experience.

- **Chores**—Experience has taught effective parents the importance and value of chores. From day 1 (or soon thereafter) children in their homes are given age-related chores, which the child is expected to fulfill. Pick up your blocks. Put away your clothes. Set the table. Mow the lawn. In ordered progress the tasks gain complexity. There are no laggards in the homes of effective parents. Effective parents do not believe laziness should be cultivated or even allowed. In their eyes it is a selfish act that needs correcting. Effective parents intentionally teach cooperative effort, the kind that not only gets work done but builds relationships.

To that end our brighter parents do more than give directions to their children like some maharajah. They roll up their sleeves and pitch in, working side by side with their children. Because they know that joint tasks bond all who have a part, the rule in their homes is that no one is done until everyone is done. Their approach to chores will surely be part of the remembering their children will do years later. At the very least it will become another layer of lacquer that deepens the family sheen and adds luster to the family memory.

- **Variety**—Lest you think I am presenting one variety of mom and dad who blindly follows a programmed approach to parenting, let me share more that I learned about effective parents.

First they were not a "they" in many instances. Some great effective parents are without partners. They are single parents. I'm not talking about only one here or one there. There are many effective single parents. Sad to say, we must add to the category of single parents another large number who are forced to function as single parents. Maybe they have a partner who is unable or unwilling to help out. Maybe their marriage is in disarray. Maybe, for multiple reasons, the "other half" is gone most of the time. Whatever, none of that precludes children growing up in an effective family. It's harder to maintain an effective home by yourself, but not impossible. So hang in there. One parent can do it. I've got a lot of letters to prove it!

Oh, yes, the world of effective parents spans the income ranges, exists in a rural-suburban-urban environment, comes in all skin tones, and prospers from coast to coast and border to border. There is only one characteristic that is constant with all: a desire to be the best mom and dad of which they are capable. On that all agree.

- **Listening**—How do you become that kind of parent? In unison, as if they were a speech choir, effective parents answer with very specific advice: Listen. When effective parents are stumped they fall back on listening as their way out. Oh, they listen at other times too. Actually they listen all the time. But their listening intensity ratchets up a notch or two when things seem to be going awry.

  They are listening for two things: (1) A clarification of the issue so that they can understand what is going on and (2) whether the children might be working out the problem themselves, without parental direction. Listening is not something to do while waiting for a chance to pour out a parental solution.

Listening is a key part of the solution. Every competent counselor knows how that works. Good listeners often nod encouragement as clients present their problems and draw their own conclusions (which they had come to the counselor to avoid). The irony is that when the process is completed, the client often profusely expresses appreciation for the help. And help it was! Listening.

Please don't think effective parents don't give explicit guidance and direction. They do. But, they hold it in check against the clear possibility that their child might work things out very well "all by myself." If, even when some outside advice is required, the period of listening makes the advice easier to take. That's what effective parents wrote to me. Their approach made sense to me. To you?

- **Forgiveness**—Effective parents are not silent when words of confession or apology are appropriate or when words of forgiveness ought to be spoken. They spend a lot of time in the world of forgiveness—and they like it there. They don't dole out cheap grace to their children any more than our heavenly Father does to us. Mistakes, offenses, errors must be faced. Effective parents understand and appreciate the point our teachers made about letting kids get by without facing the consequences of decisions. But there is always a world of reconciliation beyond that—and a way to get there.

The way to reconciliation is through forgiveness quickly offered. But it is offered *after* the cause has been properly confronted and as proper restitutions are being made. Parents who shield their children from natural consequences do more than that. They slam the door to authentic forgiveness and a chance to bring the matter to a conclusion. Those children who choose to misbehave *need* forgiveness. That can only come by facing their error and making appropriate restitution. Then comes forgiveness, a wonderful gift best given and received within a family. It's a life-giving process—especially since God, in His Word, presents forgiveness given and forgiveness received. Which leads to that great Christian word, faith.

- **Faith**—Faith is the foundation on which everything to this point—and which will follow—rests. Faith is so much more than a one-day-a-week area of interest, or a philosophy of hope built on the premise that people are inherently good. It is a view that sees everything as coming from the hand of a creating and preserving God. That God bridged the chasm separating human condition from human need. He did this in the life, death, resurrection, and ascension of His Son, Jesus Christ, who not only saves us, but by the Holy Spirit gives us power to accept the reconciliation between Him and us. That, in turn, helps us effect reconciliation between us and others, in the family and outside. There. I said it! Effective parents take that very complex sentence and apply it to every situation in which they find themselves as parents or as persons. They are very spiritual folk. And their homes exude their faith.

If you don't have this faith, you need it. How? Ask for the Lord's power in your life and His guaranteed renewal of everything you are and all that you hold dear. Ask. He gives to those who do. Promise (His promise, not mine).

- **Two kinds of moms**—One last effective parenting reality: working mothers. It could have fit under other categories, but effective parents brought it up so much that it deserves special attention. It is the only area in which there is no agreement. Some feel it is good for mothers to work outside the house. Some feel it is bad. And, of course, there are many other positions between those two extremes. I finally concluded that what they were saying was, "As far as I am concerned, it would be (a) good or (b) bad for me to work." Some chose "a." Some chose "b."

Which is right? What do you think? I think both are. My reading was that whichever stance they took, it was done after they had weighed the circumstance in which they found themselves. I could develop no general rule. Each parent, in each home, under specific conditions, came to a conclusion and then applied it in the light of their family need.

So, there you have it: concerns of effective parents. Keep them in mind as we move back to our more specific concern, effective parenting during the school daze. Match these important and helpful voices of parents to the three pointed observations of teachers that we have presented and to the six yet to come.

We'll start with one that is at the core of life for all of us: self-esteem.

Liking Who You Are

A number of years ago I co-authored a book for and about teens. Not much was being published on that subject then, and we found none that affirmed them as people. Adolescence was viewed as a dreary intermission in life that adults had to suffer. In response to that depressing attitude my co-author, Dr. Donald R. Bardill, and I titled our book, *Thank God I Am a Teenager* (Augsburg, 1988). We lifted up the many reasons for the title to be a proper theme statement for those in their teens.

The years have passed. Our book is now more than 20 years old, still available in a revised version. Why? One reason is that, aside from a little shaping here and sanding there, the core concerns of teenagers haven't changed. We know because over the years we've received thousands of letters, notes, and comments from teens. The issues haven't changed. The number one teen concern of the 1970s is still the number one concern of the 1990s: self-worth. And you know what? I believe that if my grandson writes for teens in the next century, self-esteem will be their number one concern.

Of course, most teens did not come at this self-esteem from the positive side. Few said, "It is important that I have a positive estimation of myself!"—even though it most certainly is. They come at self-esteem through the back door, the dark side of self-worth, saying, "I don't like who I am!" I-don't-like-who-I-am is nothing more than the flip side of self-worth. Both have a great effect on every one of us. It's hard to overstate the lifelong burden that a low self-image dumps on those who let it happen. In the same sense it's hard to overestimate the value of having a proper and positive sense of self.

Those few sentences about self-esteem are not just my opinion. They are repeated by every counselor, teacher, writer, and student of the human condition—at every age level, with no exception—that I have ever studied. A positive self-image is not the same as egotism any more than love is the same as lust. A properly elevated sense of self is a positive characteristic. It is claiming acceptance of one's authentic worth. It is an appreciation of what you are.

Even if a proper sense of self were not recognized by anyone in the fields of human development, it would still be enormously significant to Christians, for Scripture uses self-esteem as the measure of love. From Leviticus to Luke—with specific other citations in the gospels of

Matthew and Mark, plus Paul's letters to Rome and Galatia thrown in for good measure—the directive is repeated, "You shall love your neighbor as yourself!" That standard is mentioned so often, and so explicitly repeated in so many different places, that it is clearly a *major* theme of God's Word. More.

Variations of this emphasis can be found in almost every book of the Bible. The repetition alone makes it clear we are called to wring the best meaning possible from such an oft-repeated theme. We can't be satisfied with casually noting that it is a call to love our neighbor. It is that—and much more than that. While a scriptural call to love our neighbor would mean that we should have a positive relationship toward those about us, it is not an excuse for making lists of ways we can love—and of who ought be included in the term *neighbor*. Jesus talked to a lawyer who was into that approach in Luke 10:25–37. If we acted like that lawyer, we'd soon be so entangled in definitions of the word *neighbor* and lists of how to love that we'd miss God's easily understood standard of loving: " ... as yourself."

"As yourself." That means that we should love ourselves. And why not? With whom, by God's intent, do I spend more time? Whose destiny has greater effect on me and is more in my hands? On whose behalf do I exert more energy and offer greater protection? There is nothing wrong with a healthy, proportioned use of the personal pronouns "I" and "me." Those are powerful and essential words. People who do not use them, or who do not know how to use them, are in deep trouble. Why? More often than not, depression stems from low self-esteem and from a base sense of self. Those characteristics contribute to any number of other physical and emotional illnesses. The ultimate denial of worth is suicide and any of the other abusive excesses that surround us in society today. Nowhere in Scripture does it say I must despise myself in order to function at the highest level of God's intent for me. Actually just the opposite is true. The more I recognize, appreciate, and accept who and what God has made me, the easier it is for me to develop a properly proportioned sense of self in my service to Him. But that's not all "as yourself" implies. It calls us to the high ground of caring.

Assuming you know who you are—and whose you are—the door swings wide to an expanded measuring of the worth of others. At the same time God gives us the energy to translate concept into reality. I mean, when He leads me to see how much He trusts me, I grow in my sense of personal worth and then transfer those feelings of worth to others. When I believe in me, I can believe in you. When I recognize what I need to live the fullest life, I recognize that you need the same things as well. When

God wanted us to have a reliable criteria for helping others, He imbedded it in us. We are a kind of compass with a true north: our sense of self-worth.

So what does that have to do with parenting elementary school children? Everything! Based on—and proceeding from—your sense of self-worth you help your son or daughter develop theirs. A child equipped with a good sense of self is ready for anything life can bring, both good and bad. But young people with low self-esteem let themselves be used and abused by others. Many even invite self-abuse, believing it's no more than they deserve. Sexual deviation, drug use, and alcoholism are products of more than temptation. Those demeaning excesses seed and grow in the sour soil of low/no esteem. That's why gangs are so effective. To young people with low/no self-esteem they offer a group acceptance based not on valued achievement but on passive acquiescence to low goals and a willingness to be used. That's so different from the young woman who years ago told me how she dealt with people who pressured her to do things she felt were wrong. She would say, "I can't do that—it wouldn't be right for me."

So how can we help our kids? How can we elevate their sense of self. Answer? Give it to them. Most people gain the capacity to recognize and treasure personal worth from their homes. It is not an attribute that only life's better ones manage to develop. It is a homemade gift, usually passed on by a parent in and through the family. A few others receive it as an added benefit of someone's friendship. But regardless of the source, the elementary school years are your child's prime time for developing self-worth—and a parent's best time for teaching it. By the time elementary school days are past, most kids have their values in place, for better or for worse. A major eruption later in life, a spiritual transformation, or a powerful friendship might improve things, but unless something like that happens, there's not much hope for the full life. Not for the kids who never realized their importance.

But how? How, specifically, does a parent help proper self-esteem happen? Is it even possible to stir up that blessed attitude in our children? The answer is an emphatic yes! So say our teachers, who not only give affirmation but offer a five-part strategy for making it happen. Let the teachers teach you.

- **Let children get about the business of growing up.**

  It's not as if you can stop the process. No one has that much control because God did not give parents that option. If He had, I'm sure many parents would freeze their child at this level or that, depending on their parental comfort level. Look around: So many moms and dads are doing their very best to cocoon their children, almost hoping their little darlings will be children forever. Dependable and manageable, of course. So they hope. And act. But it is not to be. Time marches on. Teachers want parents with a yen for effectiveness to know that:

1. *Children of different ages need different privileges. Make sure each child gets his or her due no matter how younger ones may object.* In other words make sure that each child has room in which to grow unrestrained by artificial limitations.

2. *Accept your child for what he or she is. There is no mold into which any child fits best. Tailor your expectation to what your child is, not what you would like him or her to be.*

3. *Children do not need to be twisted to fit your ideal pattern. Let them grow at their own rates.*

From those three comments, and many similar ones that our teachers offered, a number of important understandings begin to evolve.

One understanding is that childhood is a dynamic time. Change is not only a reality but a necessity. Does that mean children ought to be allowed to do whatever they wish? Not at all! But they probably ought to be allowed to do considerably more than most of us, as parents, feel comfortable about. They need to stretch their wings. And parents need to help them do it.

A second understanding is that parents are to help growth happen, not to inhibit it. The parental role is usually that of the careful, but distant, watcher. Children have to walk their own way. Parents wait for the precious moments when help is appropriate and possible. One area of watchful help is making sure we do not treat all the children in the family alike. Each deserves and needs his or her individual attention and room in which to explore and discover. Some need more, some less. But all need some.

And if they aren't given parental breathing room? They'll experiment anyway, only their experimentation will take place under the control of this world's "users," far from your loving support. It may make you feel better to think the children are not experimenting with all kinds of things, but that attitude of ignorance about your child's crises is tragic. Parents are supposed to know about the stages of their children and be ready to help. They are supposed to have some anticipation of what their children will face so that they can aid them in the growth experience.

Now, before some readers become apoplectic, yes, parents ought to protect their children from temptations that are clearly more than they can handle. Drag your child out of dens of iniquity. Do it. Make decisions for them that their age makes impossible for them. There *are* times you ought and must say no. Do it. But parents will have to do less dragging, less deciding, and less "no-ing" if they decide that their primary role is in helping their child make the decision to avoid these crises *on their own.* As a matter of fact, that's what, "Train a child in the way he should go" (Prov. 22:6) means. Every child in training must experiment. They must try out the new. Most of it happens at the dangerous edge of their experience and knowledge. But supported by the watchful presence of effective parents these children are quite safe—far enough away to feel free, near enough at hand to be helped. That doesn't mean parent's hearts aren't often in their throats. Simeon's ominous words to Mary that "a sword will pierce your own soul too" (Luke 2:35) are words of doleful prophecy for modern moms and dads too. Parenting is a high-risk business filled with a potential for awesome agony. But that's not the whole of it. There's so much more joy, put there by God within His broadest intention for you and your child of the moment. Claim your joy by letting them claim theirs.

• Affirm! Affirm! Affirm!

What is there about parents that causes them to either bubble on and on about their children's accomplishments or never to say a positive thing to, or about, their kids? Of the two the latter is by far the most common. Parents who ramble on an on about their daughters and sons are quickly identified as boring deceivers and are avoided. But the grumblers about their young have many friends. Why? The more negative things we say about our children the better others feel about theirs.

Instead of either useless extreme, another possibility calls out to us. We can affirm. We can speak the good word. We can see the better possibility. So say elementary schoolteachers who yearn to share things with us about your children and mine.

1. *Tell your child you care for them. Say so clearly. Be honest in your comments. Do it often.*

2. *Look for the good in your child. Notice and compliment even the approximations to their goal. Get excited about little steps rather than save all your praise for the finish line.*

I find that second comment especially meaningful. The notion of recognizing "approximations to their goals" is wonderful and so to the point. Too often parents seem to suggest that the only tolerable standard for their children is perfection. Nonsense. If God felt that way toward us we'd all be doomed. Matthew tells us that God will not snap the weakened reed or snuff the smoldering wick (Matt. 12:20). He is the God of the Second Chance. Neither Jesus nor effective parents will pinch out tiny sparks that are trying to become something better. Rather they huff away trying to blow any embers to full flame. How?

3. *Praise as well as correct—in equal measures.*

4. *Be positive—your child's best supporter.*

5. *Especially encourage your children when their work is not so great. Never put your child down in front of others. You can't build up by tearing down.*

I'm afraid many moms and dads can't understand those five educators. One easily discernable reason for their blindness is that they do not feel affirmation themselves. Not at work. Not among friends. Not in their marriage. Of those three arenas of life we have little control over the first two—maybe change jobs or find some better friends. But as an effective parent I have a lot of control over the last. I can look for the positive in my partner and, in so doing, bless not only my spouse, but my child as well. How? In discovering flecks of goodness in my spouse I am honing the same skills needed to identify good things in my child. Look at it from the other side: Learning the importance of affirming will not only improve your effective parenting abilities but your marriage as well. Set your personal goal to find the better in your spouse and children. Tell them about it. Affirm them. It's the right thing to do. And guess what. As my North Carolina friend puts it, "You gits what you gives." My best friend says the same thing in Luke 6:38.

- **Encourage them to make an effort.**

Remember that I asked the teachers to be practical and tell me what they hoped parents would know about their elementary school children? They did some philosophizing, but not much. They did some preaching, but not much. They wrote some abstract essays, but not many. Most of all, they did what I asked. They spelled out what would help. Here are four practical suggestions for parents, all important for helping a child develop self-worth. The first is bare bones basic.

1. *Take an interest in things that seem to interest them. Watch for opportu-*

nities to help them develop these special interests. All children need a hobby.

Didn't I say they were practical? Don't try to meet your child at the point of what you like to do. Meet them at places they find fascinating. If you work at it, you might mesh your interest and theirs!

2. *Students who set reasonably high goals will achieve a reasonably high sense of success. Students who set low goals will experience feelings of low success.*

Here is where affirming gets involved. The way to elevate their goals is through affirmation. Urge them on—a little at a time, of course.

3. *Don't expect your child to be happy all the time. All people go through disappointments, deal with rejection, and face problems as they grow. Assure your child that the matter at hand can be faced. Be ready to help with advice and assistance, but do not make their problems your own.*

Wash away the tears. Apply a Band-Aid to the scrape. Give them a kiss. Pat them on the rear and send them back outdoors to take another whack at life.

4. *Sometimes it is better to overlook a minor problem in order to make sure it doesn't get confused with a major one. All problems are not alike.*

Comments 3 and 4 coalesce at the point of each one's last thought: (a) do not make their problems your own, and (b) all problems are not alike. I'm not sure which point antecedes which. Both pop up around effort—when you, or your child, exert effort you will meet these two realities. These thoughts have lifelong application but are particularly applicable to the young. Help them see this by realizing that the focus of concern is theirs, not yours. Second, recognize that all problems are not cut out of the same cloth. With that in mind, you can be that supporter who is ready to help them define the issues and cheer them on as they face it.

- **Remember: Sometimes everyone is an island.**

One of the hardest things for effective parents is knowing when to leave your child alone. John Donne's great quote that "no man is an island" is 99.44% true, but there are precious moments when we are islands. In those moments we feel like we are alone and need private time for gathering strength, courage, and understanding. Your child's closed door is not always bad. How do parents know when these private times are important?

One easy way to know is by asking. The direct question is still as fine a way to discover truth as any I know.

A second way is to observe. If you have a history of sometimes standing aside and watching, you will sense with some accuracy whether you ought to intercede. And if you are confused? Go back to the first suggestion. Ask.

Private time ought to be allowed and encouraged in the years of childhood because it is in later life. A smart teacher wrote: *Children should feel good about themselves. They need some independence. They should have responsibility. Parents can help all three happen.*

The three sentences of that quote capture much of what it means to be an adult. Childhood is the period when, by God's plan, the seed of each person is planted and nurtured to first life. Parents are there to help, not control, as steps toward maturation take place. Another teacher writes: *No matter how much a parent wants to change a child, the decision to do so is finally the child's. We'd be a lot happier if we weren't forever clashing with a child over what we think he or she ought to be and do.*

That's true. But there's a wonderful alternative to clashing. We can train them. Training our children begins with recognizing that they already have worth—as children of God, redeemed by His Son's sacrifice on the cross. We, as parents, strive to combine the best that is in them with the best that is in us in such a way that they hardly know we've been parenting effectively. They may think they were an island. One day we can tell them the island was populated by others who intentionally moved like shadows and wisps of smoke.

- **Keep at it.**

The sainted Pastor Rudolph Ressmeyer of Baltimore used to say, "The work of the church is being everlastingly at it." So true. But then so is almost everything else in life that has value. One of our teachers reminds all effective parents of this by saying, *"Don't give up on your child. Keep at it."*

There are times when a parent must give up a parental role. In a sense some of that happens when a child goes to school or joins the Scouts. We turn them over to another for help in a specific area. Even then, teachers tell us to be very sure we don't delegate interest in our child when we temporarily delegate some limited responsibilities to them. There is no voice that can buoy your children more than yours.

Even if we feel compelled to seek advice and assistance from other parents, from counselors, or from other professionals, our continued care must be felt. Parents must say, again and again, "I'll never give up on you. Never." When a child hears that, and sees actions that underpin those words, he or she knows they have value and worth. First, from God. Then, from you. Finally, from themselves. That's how they become worthwhile for others.

We need to communicate that—and so much else—to them. That art of communication is what the next chapter's about.

Listening, the Key to Communication

Words have always fascinated me. I'm not just enamored by the sound of syllables intertwining consonants and vowels, but the roots on which words build. Of all the languages none is more fascinating, complex, and filled with good roots than English. I obviously am not alone in my feelings. "The Story of English" was a hit series on the Public Broadcasting System and the title of a 1986 Viking Press book. Both are still available and will likely remain so even though English had such a modest and unpromising beginning.

When Julius Caesar landed in England 2000 years ago, English was unknown. Five-hundred years later about as many people spoke English as speak Cherokee today. Even at the time of Shakespeare, English was the spoken language of only five to seven million people in the world. Now, at the end of the 20th century, it is the mother tongue of 375 million people and has become the most widely spoken language in the history of the world.

Over the years it has developed the largest and richest vocabulary in the world with 500,000 words listed in its largest dictionary, not counting an estimated half million other uncatalogued technical and scientific terms. When compared with the German vocabulary of 185,000 words and the French vocabulary of less than 100,000, English is in a class all its own with an incredible capacity for expression.

Now don't get nervous. I haven't gone berserk. This chapter is not to be a discourse on language, language usage, or language development. We still focus on effective parents and their children. But the specific concern of this chapter is how the two use our rich language resource as they converse with each other and try to communicate.

Converse and communicate. They are not the same words. Converse means "turn together," as do ballroom dancers or a skating pair, synchronizing their rhythmic movements. Only words are used instead of intricate steps or breathtaking leaps. And communication? You can almost see its meaning in the word. See the "common?" It's there. Our ancestors believed that when two people held a common understanding, however that may happen, they were communicating.

Back for a moment to the development of the English language. The reason English is a richer language is that it has absorbed hundreds of thousands of words from other tongues. We took "honcho" from the Japanese, "thug" from India, "spaghetti" from Italy, and "hamburger" from Germany. But that ease of absorption is a problem too. Each word we have mentioned, plus their 500,000 friends, not only enriches the language but makes it harder to "hold in common" (communicate) or "turn together" (converse). You've heard people say, "Oh, is *that* what you meant?" or, "I didn't understand it *that* way!" What caused the confusion? Words. Think of all the possibilities for confusion hiding among those 500,000 words! Is it any wonder that teachers feel working at good communication is one of the most important things parents do with their children in the elementary school years?

Who agrees with them? Everyone, really. The effective parents, whose insights undergird this whole series, cry out their supportive convictions. The school families for and about whom this particular book was written agree. Every observer of the family scene picks up on two crisp directives, which teachers, not wasting a word, put before parents and children alike: (1) *speak clearly*, and (2) *listen carefully*.

I can imagine those words written on a chalkboard of the schoolroom of my youth in that perfectly formed, flowing script of Miss Aufdemberg. When she erased the whole board and then wrote short sentences with large, even cursive letters, she meant it. See these two directives as placed before you by a hundred teachers, chalk in hand.

But, in the communication age, is this kind of advice really necessary? Do we have to restate the obvious, and do it again and again? Do we have to concentrate on clear speech and accurate listening? You know the answer: we do. At least, I do—for myself.

Things haven't changed. Years ago, when it was time to introduce a young person to sex, the tool often used was a well-intentioned book, titled *Why Was I Not Told?* It came in a male and a female version. What a book! I read it, but who knew what it was talking about. Such words. Only the drawings gave a hint of the subject.

Since my introduction to that book, I've come upon it again. Rereading it, I realize that even after being told what "they" thought I needed to know, I had been told very little. The language clouded the subject worse than a San Francisco fog rolling up the bay! How? They did it with words—words that intentionally confused explanations to mysterious wonders. But have no fear. It was all explained. Other boys at school told me the facts of life in words I understood perfectly. The only problem was they didn't know much.

I would guess that the author thought he was doing the right thing for parents who reluctantly recognized they ought to give some kind of information to young men who were beginning to experience their sexuality, but with no real comprehension of what it was or how it ought to be managed. Or, maybe there was a compact between adults in those days to make sure the young didn't get much information about sex for fear they might ask pointed questions about things many adults were hesitant to explain. Whatever the reason, the result was a miscommunication that sent countless young men and young women to their marriage bed as dumb as rocks, guided only by instinct and popular myths about the world of sex. It didn't need to be that way.

We can do better than that—not only about sex but about subjects such as money, marriage, career, friendship, church, or aging. We can do better than that. All we have to do is decide we want to communicate and that we will use words both we and our children will understand. Adopt a simple rule: If either you or your child doesn't know the meaning of a word that pops up in your conversation, both have the right to ask for a definition. Parents will find such a rule can bless them every bit as much as it may bless their child. The meanings of words are in constant flux.

As an example of what I mean (and assuming you can hold your emotions in check), read with your son or daughter the words on the dust jacket of one of their compact disks or audiotapes. Take the time to define with them (a) what the words mean today and, (b) what the words mean to your child. Do that *before* you reveal (c) what they mean to you. When you do, you may discover that all three understandings are at work in your conversation. You will see how hard it is to "turn together" or "hold in common" with your child. And you will have a chance to honestly discuss with your son or daughter the kind of things parents ought to be sharing with their children. Hopefully *it will be before* someone who doesn't love them, like you do, does the explaining for you—with their values and goals controlling the conversation. Communication is tough enough all by itself without confusing it further with complex words and thoughts. That's why teacher after teacher asks parents to keep the conversation with their children simple. That usually means honest too.

While we are at it, decide that you will refuse to use a big "no-no" of communication: double messages. It means what it says. Don't send two potentially conflicting messages at the same time. A favorite parental double message is the word *maybe*. What does it mean? Maybe yes? Maybe no? Maybe what? Drop into that same bucket of "words I will not use" two more beauties: "Later" and "Possibly." There are other words and longer sentences that have the same potential for twisting hopes and confusing the young. Don't use them. Commit to clarity.

But what if the truest response is actually "maybe" or "later" or "possibly?" What then?

Package the potentially double message in a lot more words—that express the reason for your hesitance, the limitations you are dealing with, and the variables you as a parent are weighing. Kids can handle all that. They may argue but they can understand. When they understand the issues, they are capable of making the same kind of adjustment to reality that you can make.

There's more to this double messaging. Words aren't the only confusers. You can project crystal clear words in a manner that would make a Shakespearean actor marvel, and still send a confusing message. How? Scowl as you speak. Be brusque. Look disinterested or pre-occupied. Children will *mis*understand. Easily. Body language is language, and half-finished sentences send a full-fledged message.

But enough theory. This is a great hands-on section of this book. You can learn by doing. For instance, set up a tape recorder at the table for a week. Tell the family what you are doing.

Record what is said. After a few stilted moments the normal patterns of conversation will take over. After the meals, listen to the results. Check out how often a person actually got an answer to the question he or she asked. Measure how often a message was misunderstood. Evaluate the clarity of conversation. Take some time with this. Keep a diary of your observations.

More: Note how often parents and children speak. Chart it by drawing a circle on a piece of paper and writing the names of family members at different points on the arc. Then start a continuous line between the speaker and whoever responds, zig-zagging back and forth around the circle noting who speaks, and to whom. And who doesn't say much. At the end of the week review the results. Using either of those little techniques a parent will develop the raw material needed to improve conversation in the family and strengthen communication.

If this seems like too much effort, consider the alternative. The time and energy you expend because of poor communication is awesome, not to mention the pain it brings. No matter how much time you give to this little study, you will get back at least a 100% improvement in communication effectiveness in your home. At least. And you will save, in the long run, at least twice the time that making this effort requires. At least.

Folks who understand the importance of good communication that is simple and clear actually take courses in communication. Almost every community offers them. If you don't know where to turn, talk to your child's teacher. You'll get help there. In addition there are good books such as *Renewing the Family Spirit* by Dr. David Ludwig. By whatever means, take the time to develop your capacity for clearly presenting your ideas and clearly understanding the words your children say.

We've gotten a lot of mileage in this chapter out of the two comments teachers made about clarity and simple words. The comments deserve every bit of that attention. There are three other simple admonitions from teachers that are tied to communication. All are short, but so important.

- **Avoid put-downs.**

Calling a third-grader "a baby" or "dumb" or "selfish like your father" plugs up ears. The same goes for all the other K–6 kids. Look in a mirror. The same teasing words and ways that are tough enough on adults are super destructive on the very young who have no experiences for evaluating the significance of demeaning comments. Words that belittle the listener severely inhibit communication. Simply put: Don't say about your children things you wouldn't want your boss to publicly say about you.

What's awesome about this point is that the adult speaker has full control in this matter! There's no external compulsion that requires adults to use scornful or mocking language. Quite the contrary. By the time you are an adult, you ought to know from experience how derision affects the ego of most and how ineffective it is as a motivator. Those who feel compelled to use put-downs not only make problems—but apparently have one as well. Both observations need attention.

• **Pick the best place to talk.**

The characteristics of a "best" place to talk with your child include: (a) it is private, (b) the surroundings are quiet, (c) the moment is unhurried, and (d) the atmosphere is friendly. Judging from the letters I received from effective parents, few places stir up good conversation better than the kitchen table. The bedroom is good too, especially at bedtime. Leisurely walks help words flow for many. The point the teachers want to make is that when you want to have a good chat, choose the place it happens as carefully as the words you use. The place gives texture to the words you want to share.

Years ago another great teacher taught me, "Try never to make serious corrections just before bedtime. The dark night and a bad conscience make a poor twosome." He would add to the suggestions of today's teachers, "Pick the best place, *and the best time,* to talk." Either way, take control.

- **Nothing helps communication like feedback.**

Sound a bit sophisticated to you? Maybe. But it is today's parlance, understood by most. The point is that when it's important to you or your child, be sure the conversation does not end without asking the child to "feed back" to you what you said. You can start the process yourself by doing what you want your son or daughter to do. You might begin by saying, "Now, if I understand correctly, you are saying to me that ...." Keep working at defining the conversation until your child agrees that you have understood his or her message. Then answer. Say what you feel you have to say, but don't go your separate ways until your child gives the same kind of feedback to you. You may not be famous for clarity of speech, but who cares? If the child didn't receive the message you sent, the process must be repeated until communication takes place.

And, of course, it may be feasible that the fullest communication is not presently possible on *that* topic. It may require postponing the chat to a specific later time, giving both of you a chance to find clarity. Both. Communication and conversation require that both speak clearly so that understanding is possible. Which leads to our teachers' other shoe: "Listen carefully," they say in chorus.

I've primarily been dealing with the easier and more obvious part of conversation and communication to this point: speaking clearly. There is another part that is at least a 50% slice, though I believe teachers and other effective parents would list it as a 90%. I'll let six teachers, from six schools teaching six different grade levels, lay the groundwork. Then we can pick around in their quotes critical understandings.

1. *Show your children that you are listening to them.*
2. *Take time to listen to your children. Ask them about their school day. Find out what is important to them.*

134

3. *Treat your children with respect. Listen to them. Consider their feelings. Weigh their opinions.*
4. *Be willing to listen to your children. Most of the time no answer is required.*
5. *Talk with them. Listen to your children. Eye to eye.*
6. *Listen. You don't have to make every conversation a teaching time. Sometimes just listen. Ask an opinion. Try to discover who this child is—what he or she dreams about—likes and dislikes—feels—has as goals. Appreciate the uniqueness of each child.*

Digging around among those great suggestions surfaces a number of important matters. One important thought is that parents ought to listen to their children. Of course, children ought to listen to parents. But this book isn't for children; it's for parents. One way that listening is taught to children is by practicing with them what you want from them.

Listening—how do you do that? At the very least it requires eye-to-eye contact—focused attention. When the issue feels very important, put down whatever you have in hand and concentrate on them and their message. Look at them. Listen to their whole speech without comment or interruption. When they are done, first give them your feedback. Before an answer. The feedback is to assure the speaker that you have received the message they sent. Nothing more, but certainly nothing less. Included in this feedback you can properly try to ferret out what they would hope from the conversation. Are they only giving information? Are they seeking help? Are they trying out an idea that they want to use somewhere else? Are they just thinking out loud? Make sure you know their intention and be sure that they know you know. Eye-to-eye contact helps that happen.

What if you don't have a good answer or aren't sure which good answer you ought to give? Don't give a hurried response. Say something like: "Thank you for trusting me enough to tell me this. I want to share with you the very best that I have. Could you let me think about this for a while? Would it be all right if we discussed this again on Friday, after I've had a chance to gather my thoughts and weigh out the best response I can develop?" Unless the matter of conversation is an emergency (it sometime is, but not often), a response like that will only assure your son or daughter that you care and that you are not taking their concern lightly. It will also give you the very thing asked for: time.

So what do you do with that time? Use it. Read about the matter at hand or discreetly consult with another whose judgment you trust or who could give you the kind of additional information that you need. Perhaps you just want time to think and weigh alternatives. Many of us as adults are too quick with our opinions. Things have changed in significant ways since we were children. Test the changes before you speak.

My dad didn't believe we should go to movies on Sunday. When he was a child in another era, attending a Sunday movie sent a very different message. That little speck of an illustration only hints at the enormity of change that has taken place since you hiked the road your child now treads. The principles do not change, but the applications sure do. Fight for a little time to sort things out. Truth will not deteriorate while you pause to reflect; but good advice can often improve with a little aging.

Remember, again, the premise on which this section is built: The most essential part of conversation and communication is listening. The better you can "hear," the more likely you will be able to help. To test your hearing go back and review the six comments from teachers. Underline some of the key words and thoughts. Which ones fit you and your child best? Note them at the end of this chapter.

Then ask your child for help. Tell them that you want to improve communication with them and others. Tell them that you need practice. Ask them to work with you five minutes a day.

Isolate five minutes after school (or around a meal) in which, on one day, you ask them about their day at school. The next day you talk to them about what you have been doing. End each session with a minute or so of feedback.

Let me suggest what will happen. At first the process may be strained and unnatural. The children may be suspicious, especially if you haven't been an attentive listener before. But keep at it. Recognize and admit a conversational weakness. What will start out stilted and awkward will soon become normal. Both you and your children will prepare for the five minutes. Then subjects will surface of themselves. The wariness will wane and in its place will develop a naturalness that will last a lifetime: yours and theirs. And the five minutes will expand.

Good communication can start during the dazzling and sometimes dazing elementary school days. It can start if you decide it is important. Teachers say it is. Ditto for effective parents. Common sense and experience agrees with both. All that's needed is your parental decision. It's not likely your children can or will initiate a process of intentional and genuine conversation and communication. That privilege lies with you. If you decide to work together, you will set the stage for the next chapter with its marvelous accent on togetherness.

Row, Row, Row Our Boat

If schoolteachers and effective parents had not made this chapter's focus notable in the parenting of elementary school children, I would have figured out some way to wedge it in. From the day our first child was born, my wife, Audrey, and I have believed families need to do things together. We were a "we" long before Sarah entered elementary school. Together—a family. And what do the teachers think about that? They agree. They emphasize that parents, to be effective, need to do things with their children—and that the initiative lies with the parents.

Here's how they said that:

- *Become involved in your children's activities.*

- *Make time to show your love for your child. Slow down. Work with them. Try not to hurry your child.*

- *Find time to attend children's programs, games, plays, etc.—even in high school.*

- *Allow your children to share in plans for special days, trips, and times with the family. That's how they learn their input is important.*

- *Teach your child the joys of sharing. Set the example. Help them volunteer in some way.*

- *Spend time with your child. Play, learn, and talk together. Long after they've forgotten the TV show you had to see or the book you had to finish, your child will remember the time you had together.*

Those six suppositions capture the gist of what many other teachers, many other effective parents, and common sense suggest. All three urge parents to *"do things together with your children. Do it now."* But why the emphasis—almost a feeling of urgency—during the school days? One reason is the readiness of the children.

Elementary school kids are at a great intersection of life. They are so primed to cooperate. Collaborative efforts are easy to initiate and maintain during those wondrous years. The children are at a peak of adaptability, eager to do things together with you. By the time they slip into the teens, it's harder to initiate collaboration and to sustain cooperation. For many families too many years of neglect and too many missed opportunities have been racked up before age 13. "Why the interest now?" lots of kids ask. The time to build the rest of your life is now.

As Audrey and I went about raising our house full of children, we had hearts full of love, and minds brimming with creativity, but not much money. Any different than with many of you now? We decided we would not let money be the issue. With or without it we determined to do things together. But what? I've never been a hunter or a fisherman, so those activities weren't too promising. Camping didn't appeal to either of us. We went through a number of other possibilities, which either interest or income eliminated.

While mulling it over, one of us read about developing family moments, specific chunks of time dedicated to enhancing togetherness. That sounded good to us. One of our first family moments was a practical one: We initiated what became a Saturday ritual of pancakes, baths, washing and combing hair, shining shoes (I still hate saddle oxfords), and watching TV. After a pancake supper, Audrey would start soaking them in the bathroom, scrubbing them good, and shipping them on to me for drying their hair and combing out the knots. During breaks in the bath brigade, the children and I shined about a million pairs of shoes. That's the way Audrey, our three daughters, and one son got ready for Sunday school and church for nearly 18 years. We were well into our 40s before Audrey and I went out to dinner and a movie, alone, on a Saturday night. The first time we couldn't shake the feeling that something was wrong. Nothing was wrong. We were just experiencing the aftershocks of an era passing.

There was more togetherness sought and grasped in those days. I actually got involved in writing because the children didn't like devotions, responding better when their names were in them and when incidents from their lives were featured. A family Advent devotional book, first prepared for and used with them, (*The Christian Family Prepares for Christmas*, CPH, 1963) is still available today. I have no idea how many other families have used that booklet for building togetherness. I'm glad if they have. But I'm happiest that we did.

When the children got older, Audrey and I developed games to play at the supper table. In one I would riffle through our dictionary until one of our children told me to stop. Then by a process of elimination they would pick the left or right page, the left or right column, and a finally a word so many words from the top. Once selected I'd make up a story with a moral to it—or offer some limp humor—and then let them try to spell the word. If they spelled it correctly, they were excused and could leave the table. (As the father in control I always made sure the word was within their capability.) And what happened after they gleefully spelled their way away from the table? They wanted to spell their way back. What fun!

Summers were full of excitement. We capitalized on the "moonlighting" that was available to me as a pastor. It usually came in the form of being asked to speak at a summer camp with a cabin and meals for the family in lieu of compensation. Not bad! I worked some. Audrey escaped a week of cooking. The kids had a riotously good time. And we had fun driving the thousand or more miles to this place or that, inventing games and stopping at motels with swimming pools! I can hear, "Are we there yet?" even as I write.

Evenings were out for me. As a pastor I used them for making calls on people. No one wants to see a pastor late in the afternoon so I happily traded evenings for late afternoons and was usually home when the four bounced in from school. Often as not I picked them up. We lived just less than the mile required to qualify for riding the bus. If it wasn't ride-with-me, it was walk-for-them. They liked my taxi. It gave us talk time.

School was the focal point of our together-ness, especially on the rare occasions when things had gone a little awry in their world. When things were less than positive, Audrey or I went to school so that we might face the music together with our little ones. In those moments when they were down, they didn't need lec-tures. They needed love and our reassuring presence. When the music had been faced, about all we asked was, "Is this all over now? Are we done with doing things that way?" Their nod was the end of the matter for us. I can't remember ever dealing with the recurrence of a problem that took us to the darker side of school life. If there had been one, we'd have handled it the same way. But there wasn't. I think it's because we made even the less tasteful parts of life a matter of family togetherness that we all could put behind us and get on with life.

Most of the things that took us to school were happy, bright things: awards, contests, plays, sports, musical efforts. We didn't miss much. Not long ago Audrey told me the only regret she had was that she never saw our son play football in high school. I told her she hadn't missed much. While he was on the team and showed great courage in hanging in there, his career lasted about two plays. I saw them both. She missed about 45 seconds. Had he been a foot taller, and 50 pounds heavier then, it would have been a different matter. What fascinates me about her comment is that after all these years Audrey still has that little twinge. I think she is saddened because she missed a mighty family moment. That gives me additional insight into the heart of a mother who believes in doing things together.

Paper routes? *We* had them. Babysitting all kinds of people and things that need babysitting? *We* sat them. *We,* together, raised dogs through all the stages of "I promise to feed him every day" to "do I have to?" *We* did it. All of us. *We* specialized in turtles, fish, and parakeets too. I'm not sure how much all this taught them about responsibility and duties and work. But *we* all learned a lot about love and togetherness and helping each other out.

Our peak seasons of family togetherness were the couple days before Easter, Christmas, and Halloween. The first two were much more Audrey's days than mine. She sewed. For most of our early years I dozed off every holy day eve with the whir of Audrey's sewing lulling me to sleep. Come morning light on the festal days, miraculously, all the dresses were finished, hanging in the doorway. We did laugh that if any of the girls had sneezed hard they would have been left standing there in their slips!

Halloween was a joint effort—togetherness personified. We bought no costumes. We believed that we could create anything the kids wanted out of cardboard, wire, paint, and cloth—together. And we did. Some were marvels of engineering. Even today I drop a little something extra into the sack of any trick-or-treater who comes to our door in a clearly homemade costume. I hope they save some of their loot for those back home who helped them. Our kids did.

So what do Audrey and I have to show for all this effort? Have the children grown up aware of what we did, knowing how much we both intentionally put into our family? I'm not sure. Nor do we expect it. That memory belongs to the two of us. The authentication of what we did is not in their memories but in what they are naturally doing for and with their children. All our grown children are "togetherness" parents, who have married "togetherness" spouses. I'm pleased at how much they do for the young—whether it be their own, those of their extended family, or someone else's kids. I don't expect them to stand around admiring those who taught them this style of relationship any more than Audrey and I stood around admiring those who taught us.

And someone did. Audrey and I think it was our parents, Rudolph and Augusta, Walter and Aurelia. In my mind's eye, I can go back to the togetherness school I attended as a child in Kansas. I see my mom and dad, my brother and sisters. Audrey finds the same history of strong family togetherness in her Arkansas roots, plus what flowed out of the wonderful house on Beethoven Street in South St. Louis. There was always room for another and a hand to help anyone, family or not. We were trained for parenting by some outstanding teachers. Did we ever tell them how they affected us? No, but we did better than that—we imitated them.

With my background, the teachers' sentences were more than congenial suggestions to my way of thinking. They highlighted a super-highway to parental effectiveness that can be traveled even while the children are in grade school. Any parent with a yen for effective parenting will find in these teachers' comments a master plan of action, plus broad comments about what is needed to move to a higher level of care. What's needed to move up is not complicated nor difficult. It appears what's needed are four understandings.

- **Understanding 1: Parent and child must find a common page.**

Now that's not unreasonable, is it? Both parent and child need to be involved in doing the same thing at the same time. Parental effectiveness is not built on the child watching from a distance as you do your thing—or as you watch them do theirs. There needs to be a commonality of action, hopefully simultaneous. A wonderful illustration is found in the choirs I enjoyed in many of the Black churches while serving among them in the '70s. I never found a children's choir in those Carolina congregations. There was just "a choir" with those who wanted to sing. Whole families, from grandma to grandson, made music together. The participation was not based on age but on kinship and desire to be together. As I thought about it, that approach took on a beauty all its own. It was like all the dads and moms who bond beautifully with their sons and daughters in Little Leagues of all kinds for almost every sport. Sure there are parents who lose control in these events and overwhelm the moment with their presence. But not most. Most are out there building memories of parental interest and support for their children's tomorrow and for their own.

Organized sports or musical groups are not the only doorway to developing common interests. There's a doorway of hobbies and crafts where age is not as significant as interest. There is the doorway of the great outdoors, of gardening, of reading, of associations such as the Scouts, 4-H, and church youth groups. There are doorways between generations everywhere. All that's needed is a desire to find some common ground between you and your child—and, of course, a willingness to lay aside the supposed "marks" of parenthood: infallibility, power, unquestioning obedience. Those things don't build family togetherness. Better relational tools are discussion, sharing views, asking advice, working toward agreement. Those are the things that allow you and your child to be on the same page.

- **Understanding 2: Time, unlike money, is a commodity that will only be spent and cannot be saved.**

Harry Chapin's provocative song, "Cat's in the Cradle" is a sobering reminder of Understanding 2. Remember the lyrics? A son asks his dad to join him in one life event after another, while the father verbalizes a spirit of caring, but is distracted by his own needs and never quite accepts the invitation. Instead the dad keeps saying, "I don't know when I'll be home, but we'll get together then, son; we'll get together then." In the last verse the dad is old and wants to talk with the son who's now grown. The son can't seem to make time available for his father—and feeds back the same line that he received as a child: "I don't know when I'll be home, but we'll get together then, dad;—we'll get together then."

The years of your child's growing are of predictable length, barring a tragic shortening of his days—or yours. And then your son or daughter is gone, if not physically, at least emotionally. The saying that "time and tide wait for no man" is a powerful truth as well. Parental windows of opportunity move relentlessly toward closure. Knowing this is true is not the same as understanding that it is true. Understanding stirs to action. And action is what our children need.

- **Understanding 3: There must be a decision.**

That word *decide* is one of those wondrous English words that was built in another language and imported into ours. It comes from the same Latin root as the word *scissors*. And right there you have it: Scissors cut. So do decisions. As scissors slice their way through fabric, hair, and rope, decisions slash through opportunities and challenges. Something that is cut cannot be completely restored. There will always be a weakness that indicates where the cut took place. But who cares? Cuts are not made so that the old condition can be restored. They are made so that new things can be created. Effective parents know. They decide. They cut through choices and slice away at challenges, determined that something better can be brought into being. But it's always a risk.

I received many letters from dads who intentionally quit activities they enjoyed in order to be with their children in the years from four through 12 and beyond. They *decided* to do this. They made a cut that could not be restored. How does a 28-year-old-dad—who quit competitive baseball in order to be with his children in their growing years—get back into that sport at 40? He doesn't. Moms were just as intentional about rearranging their priorities. And they were just as brave and selfless.

There is no principle that covers acceptable and unacceptable decisions. Not all parents cropped their activities for their kids' sake. Some did just the opposite. They expanded their participation but made sure their kids could function as a full-fledged part of their commitment. Lots of families do that. They embark on projects in which all have ownership, whether it is running a farm, a family business, square dancing, or getting a church ready for Sunday. The whole family is involved and knows the critical role that all play. It happens that way because a decision has been made.

- **Understanding 4: After the decision comes more hard work.**

It would be lamentable to leave anyone with the impression that deciding to do something is the same as doing it. Deciding is only the beginning. Then comes the doing, when togetherness is easiest, almost automatic. Once the doing starts, the whole family gets involved in gathering the materials, constructing the boat, and floating down the river. The whole family gets to plan and take the trip, plant and harvest the garden, select and attend the movie.

The key to the process is getting everyone involved at the level of their abilities. That's almost harder than the doing, but just as important. Parents who don't quite understand this say to their kids, "Just get out of here. I'll do it myself. It's easier that way!" No doubt about it. Thirty-year-old fingers and arms can do most things easier and quicker than eight-year-old ones. But doing is not what it's all about. Doing together is the point of the exercise. Bonding is the priority. Building relationships is the goal. Bringing out what's better in your child is the objective.

Remember that this book is not about children; it's about parenting. It's not aimed at helping you get things done faster or smoother or easier. It's aimed at helping you parent better, becoming so adept that you will feel and be effective. The first to benefit from that developing effectiveness will be your child. The second will be you. The third will be your spouse. But the first one who will recognize that you are doing a remarkable job of parenting may be none of them. It will probably be the rest of us. We will sense that something wonderful is happening in your home and will comment. It happens that way. When I wrote families that they had been recognized by others as effective, almost everyone expressed surprise.

Amazing: The last to recognize effectiveness in themselves are the very ones who blaze a trail for the rest of us to follow. They do this by making sure their family members are not only linked by blood but by cooperative ventures.

Can you do the same? Easy. Don't start with a series of life-changing resolutions. Pick an activity (a trip to the zoo?) or an event (a birthday party?) or a holiday (Thanksgiving?). Determine to make it a family moment. Invite everyone to suggest things they can contribute to the chosen project. As a parent, knowing all the people involved, add to each one's suggested contribution something you know they can do and, perhaps, like to do. Enrich the event. Take at least one picture of each person doing their thing, plus at least one of everyone together. Put the pictures on the fridge. Once photos are posted, plan the next family event.

And, in the meanwhile, talk with your partner. Discuss what life adjustments each ought to make in order to have more family strengthening activities, including adventures that feature this child or that. It all builds family. And in building the family you also help each child find and set the boundaries for life.

Which is what we will consider in the next chapter.

Setting the Boundaries

There's a big world out there that doesn't support much of what Christian homes feel ought to be taught to their children. If that world supports anything positive (and there is reason to wonder whether it does), it does so for its own reasons. That's why teaching children how to live in that chaotic world environment is one of the most important things parents do.

In the world beneath the sea, where an oxygen tank and a breathing mask are essential, a scuba diver can get disoriented about something as ordinary as which way is up. Some early unsuspecting divers, not recognizing the problem, actually swam down to a watery death thinking they were swimming toward the surface. To prevent that tragedy today, diving instructors teach novices to determine up and down while under water. It's an easy lesson everyone wants to learn, once they know what's at stake.

We need to offer similar direction—protection—to our children in our homes. Only the directions that need protection are not up and down. They are right and wrong. Teaching children right from wrong is not easy. It's not even easy to consistently discriminate right from wrong. Big chunks of life seem to be shades of gray, making even the simplest choices difficult.

Establishing and teaching moral directions through standards, values, and other basic life ingredients is one of the most important tasks of parents. Even if the children later ignore the path that their parents presented, they at least know the path exists. They know there is a moral "up" and probably even know how to find it. Effective parents intentionally teach the fundamentals of morality through their own standard of living and by the conduct they press their children to understand and emulate. Elementary schoolteachers and hundreds of effective parents agree that setting moral standards is one of the most important, and most often neglected, responsibilities moms and dads have.

Compounding the problem of some parents who fail to give moral direction is a second problem that is just as serious. When some parents do give directions, the directions they give are so wrong! Three common examples of parental misdirection surfaced in a discussion with a panel of parents. These effective parents described the three moral mistakes as the following:

Misdirection 1: Take care of yourself first.

That theme, and variations of it, is being taught in homes every day. Teachers hear it from their students. What's especially troubling is that it sounds right—as if the parents were saying, "Mind your own business." Not bad advice, unless the implicit message is that we should not get involved, no matter what. Taken to extreme, that advice became the Nazi concentration camp guard's wide-eyed, "I saw nothing!"—a denial that some think frees you from responsibility. It doesn't. That denial is not the end for either the hesitant witness or the reluctant helper. His or her moment of denial is a seed from which other later outrages sprout. And the new set of injustices, with poetic evenhandedness, inevitably erodes the quality of life of the one whose head was conveniently turned away at a critical moment.

We must teach our children that it's always high noon in someone's life, somewhere in the world. Only in this scenario it's not Gary Cooper acting out his academy-award role in the face of looming evil. No. It's real live people making choices about matters that affect millions. Evil will always exist in our sinful world, and it will triumph when good men and women do nothing. People in service to others do not develop in homes that feature courses in self-interest. The pattern of heroic concern for others is laid out for them early by parents who, themselves, live lives of care and who teach it to their sons and daughters with intentionality. That's what parents say—and what effective parents say parents are for.

Misdirection 2: Charity begins at home.

The difference between this second flawed attitude and the first is that the second is active, not passive. Because it is active it's also adversarial in openly pitting "our" family's wants and needs against the wants and needs of others. The cruel distortion is that the levels of need in life are the same, family to family. In a misguided home a child's want for a private phone is treated as if it were the same as another child's hunger for enough rice to make it through the day.

When will children have a chance to decide whether their bargain-rate loafers are worth the price of hundreds of thousands of Third World children sewing shoe uppers from dawn to dusk for $1 a day? When will our children be taught how to answer the narrow greed that has the audacity to ask, "Well, if those children weren't sewing shoes, what would they be doing?" In the past nameless millions refused to be passive in the face of evil and, at great personal cost, destroyed slavery, forced the adoption of a minimum wage for millions in the U.S.A., and pulled children out of sweatshops. It's bad enough to be passive in an evil environment, but to actively encourage wickedness is appalling. If nothing else we are at least our brother's keeper. That's the minimum level of relationship. But there *is* more beyond "keeping" our brothers. We are our brother's brother and our sister's sister. *That's* the proper moral truth parents are called to teach their children at home.

If that is not persuasive enough, there are other reasons for teaching children that it is wrong to ignore the needs of others. Such callousness not only fails to help others, it endangers us by anesthetizing others toward our inevitable moments of need. And, that day comes to all. History teaches us a truth that my North Carolina friends express with such simple directness: "What goes around comes around." No one's star is in perpetual ascendancy. If a parent can think of no loftier reason for teaching the caring, nonadversarial life to their children, there is always the reality of self-interest.

Misdirection 3: Always be ready to compromise.

That sounds almost right. Or does it almost sound right? Either way, the thought implicit in that simple sentence is no value upon which your child will likely build a fruitful life.

Granted, life requires compromises. And granted, compromise is okay in areas of God-given choices. And granted, compromise can be an important life skill. But that's not the whole of it. Critical to the process for life effectiveness is clearly understanding which things cannot properly be compromised. President Lyndon Johnson's oft-quoted comment that "politics is the art of compromise" needs lots of explanation and thoughtful consideration. Many see it as a view that nothing is right or wrong. People with that attitude are in as much danger as the scuba diver who is uncertain of the way to the surface. Hardly a week goes by without a newspaper report of a businessman, sports figure, or politician who lost his bearing in the waters of life. So what can parents do to help?

At the very least, they can confront the three flawed signposts, making sure they believe, and teach, that life is more than making the best deal possible and that truth, while it is fragile, is not without form. One help for doing this is turning to our children's teachers. They have very specific directives (based on living with our children for six or more hours a day) to help us show the way.

Directive 1: Teach your children that there are boundaries.

Now that isn't hard. As a matter of fact, teaching about boundaries has to precede lessons they will learn about natural consequences. If they knew about boundaries, I wonder how many would be spared a painful natural consequence or two in life?

You don't even have to determine most boundaries. Many are set by law. (Like it or not you must go to school.) Lots fall into the category of common sense. (Don't touch fire.) Then there's the direction you get from family. (You can always go to your aunt's house if you need help.)

The boundary setter, par excellence, is God. One way to look at His boundaries is to imagine you are living on an expansive fertile plateau. The edges of the plateau drop precipitously to jagged rocks far below. To topple off the edge is to risk certain injury, even death. For your safety's sake God builds a sturdy fence along the boundary so that you can't accidentally tumble to your doom. Yet, if you are willful enough, you can climb over the fence at risk of your life. That fence? It is God's Law: the Ten Commandments (Exodus 20), the Sermon on the Mount (Matthew 5, 6 and 7), many specific teachings of Jesus (Luke 10, for example), the inspired Word to Micah (6:8) and James (1:27). And much more.

So say the teachers, with a reminder. God not only gave us His Law. He gave His only Son to fulfill that Law perfectly and take the punishment for the times we fail to keep it. That great love and the Spirit's guidance motivate us to live within His boundaries.

Directive 2: Hold your children, and yourself, to those boundaries.

I couldn't say it better than the third-grade teacher who wrote: *Agree on the boundaries that you and your child will honor, and determine what will happen if they are crossed.*

First, establish the boundary. The best ones are mutually accepted. Then show your seriousness by stating in specific terms the consequences for all concerned if those boundaries are transgressed by either of you.

I like our teachers' ways of defining things. They begin by insisting that parents initiate this process and then make sure there is a concurrence or, at the very least, a clear understanding of where those boundaries lie. Establishing boundaries calls for the interaction of parent and child, right? That's where the earlier chapters come into play. The interaction happens best when it contains elements of togetherness, listening, and understanding both yourself and your child. Without those insights and skills effective parenting will not happen.

Then, when that process has taken place, and when reasonable and acceptable rules have been put in place, one decision remains. Will the *parent* honor the limitations? The parent decides that, not the child. Parenting is a parent's task.

Directive 3: Recognize that children are experts at evasion.

When children are given opportunity, they create new rules—or no rules. Even with well-developed rules children know how to get away with things. One fourth-grade teacher wrote: *Ninety-five percent of all students are able to be responsible. However, if adults do not expect children to be responsible, they won't be.* His second-grade counterpart added: *Students are probably the smartest humans around. They know exactly what is and what is not expected. They also know the exact point where they should not be allowed to act independently of others. Parents need to know that too.*

If you have trouble recognizing that baseness in your children, consider adopting a different perspective. Instead of looking for all that human stuff in them, look for it in yourself. What the two teachers observed about the kids is what you know to be true in yourself, including the tilt toward covering up. If you can't see it in yourself, consider risking your marriage by asking your spouse whether he or she sees evasive leanings in you. If that's too risky, try asking the same of a friend or a coworker. It's there. St. Paul captures the inclination beautifully with the words, "For what I do is not the good I want to do; no, the evil I do not want to do—this I keep on doing" (Rom. 7:19). Like so many other problems of life, evasion is hereditary.

That being true it is important that parents do not excuse a tendency in their children that they came by naturally, but which left unattended can scar them for life. Parents are to also protect children from themselves. What doth it profit a mom or dad to shield their child from every enemy only to have them injured by self-inflicted wounds?

Directive 4: Let your NO be NO.

All of which sets the stage for one of the most common teacher admonitions:

Once you've set age-appropriate boundaries, learn how to say NO. And stick with it.

Put another way a teacher advises, *When you say NO, please mean it. Otherwise why say it?*

From those two comments twin suggestions arise. First, set age-appropriate boundaries. That implies setting individual child-appropriate boundaries as well. To do that you will have to know what is appropriate to children of a certain age and, specifically, what is appropriate to your child. All that studying comes first.

Before we move on, did you notice what *isn't* mentioned? Nothing is said about the social environment—what others of their age might need, or think they need. Each child is seen as unique. An impassioned, "but everyone else is doing it, has it, wants it," isn't even considered. Once *your* child's genuine needs are known; once *your* child's boundaries have been mutually set; once *your* child's situation has been weighed, the question of what others do is of little interest. Those concerns might be part of the deciding process but are irrelevant after the fact.

Then comes the heart of the matter. Let there be no wavering. Do the ground work. Weigh the matter together. Be reasonable— with you doing the adult/parent part of deciding what that word means. Be fair. Then be firm. NO means NO. A change may later be negotiated, but until that happens, the decision is the decision.

The reason teachers are so vocal on this point is that every day they deal with the spinoff of parental spinelessness: a poorly trained child. These teachers are not calling for parental inflexibility or unreasoned arbitrariness. They are encouraging a responsible decision-making process, which, once it has played out to the end, becomes the rule.

And if parents are casual in this matter? They curse their child for life. If the nutritionist who says, "We are what we eat," is correct, then the observation "As the twig is bent, the tree will grow" is correct as well. And it is. To put it simply, kids become what they are. They take the attitudes developed during childhood into their teen friendships, dating, sports, and school. Those same attitudes crop up later at college, during courting, at work, in marriage, and, in family. In all those areas they will suffer natural consequences from which no permissive or indulgent parent can save them. Learn that a reasoned NO means NO. It is an important lesson for life.

Directive 4: Start training in an easy area: the child's own world.

But when should this life training start? A first-grade teacher tells us: *Start a child's training for life as early as possible, with the basics. Expect your children to care for their belongings. Even little things such as game pieces need tending.*

If I ever questioned the age that intentional home training should begin, I became convinced that this can start at an early age the day I visited Trinity Children's Home near Gramado in southern Brazil. There are not one or two children there. There are 100 or more, of all elementary school ages. Under the loving and firm guidance of a very small staff, the older children care for themselves first, and then help tend the younger ones. Everyone has a duty. It has been explained to them in a careful and caring way. Once done, there is no evasion of responsibility. The children know what has to be done and they do it—with joy.

Can this work in your home? Certainly. Establish age-related tasks. At the earliest age, even if you work with them, insist they be a part of the task. Let them do some room cleaning, pick up toys, place some clothes in the laundry, set the table or empty the dishwasher. Whatever. But do not let their tasks accumulate. If you have to do a week's worth of cleanup on Saturday morning, the assignment can be overwhelming. Set daily boundaries like, "Cleanup must be complete before play," or "Chores come before TV." Don't think this is the largest problem in the world. Farm children have been taught responsibility for centuries. City cousins can be just as accountable if the parents establish the expectations.

Start with the simplest task. Then, in time, build.

Directive 5: School and schoolwork belong in the learning loop.

It makes sense. It is especially true since the teachers are there to help you in your task of training your children. The teachers' suggestions? Here are three:

Set homework rules.

Make school and schoolwork a priority for everyone in the family.

*Children age 9 and 10 need to be respon-
sible for things such as taking homework
back to school. Do not take it for them.*

These suggestions are logical progressions
from the earlier one of picking up game pieces.
School is a marvelous arena in which to learn
life's most important lessons under ideal and
friendly circumstances. But the parent must see
it as such. School is a transitional learning environment where the goal is not to get through
the grades as easily as possible but to move
from class to class learning as many lessons for
life as you can. To do that, recognize and intentionally implement the preceding five points.

Directive 6: Expand their horizons.

Teachers know that passing through one
grade is not the end of the educational process.
Classes come and then they go. Next year
another rowdy band of children will enter their
rooms needing the shaping that the educational
system tries to offer. By then, this year's room of
children will have graduated to the next level
in school. Then the next. And the next. Teachers also know that education is more than what
happens in the schoolroom. So it comes as no
surprise that teachers are interested in parents
helping the children broaden their horizons—
beyond their school, beyond the home. How?
One put it this way:

Allow your children to experience life in other homes. See to it that they can invite other children into yours.

That one comment is not the whole of it. Teachers are suggesting that parents look for ways to give children other experiences. As our children grew, we invited Job Corps cadets to spend weekends in our homes; we looked for ways to help them know children of other races and cultures; we tried hard to say yes to even their wilder stabs at new things; we talked with them about anything, giving explanations as long as their eyes didn't glaze over. One reason I thought new worlds were important was that as a child in Kansas I was given tickets to a series of plays which, if nothing else, introduced me to the world of theater—and writing, and reading, and speaking in public, and art, and design. And so much else. I knew there was more out there. There still is, and until your child finds that out, it will remain a hidden possibility for him or her.

Directive 7: Lead them to make—and keep—commitments.

As a kind of postscript, the teachers opened one more wondrous door to growing up. Actually it's the glue of society: commitment. Without commitment how would the institution of marriage continue? Or why would firemen fight fires at risk of life—or, policemen guard, or teachers teach, or doctors serve, or carpenters properly build parts of the house that will finally be covered and hidden? Commitment puts the Sunday school teacher in the class each week, the den leader in the Cub Scout meeting, the Little League coach into the game. A teacher writes: *Help your children fulfill commitments such as being at church on time when their choir sings or going as a prepared member of their Girl/Boy Scout troop.*

What jumps out at me in that quote are the words, "Help your child fulfill ...." The parental role is one of support. It's not one of necessarily doing things for them (though that can sometimes be called for too), but to help them do it. Helping a 12-year-old prepare for a merit badge is not all that different from helping a three-year-old pick up blocks. Accent word? Help.

But I also like two other points. First, if little kids are to be on time for anything—and that is important for them and for the people helping you with your child—they are dependant on you for transportation. Parents can help a lot by getting their child to the church/school/troop/game on time.

Second, help them arrive prepared. Very few meetings take place that do not call for some kind of preparation, whether it be a lesson completed, a proper uniform, some refreshments for the group. Parents can and should help their children be prepared. It's one of our great privileges during those wondrous elementary school daze.

As always, I'm never sure where the next chapter ought to be placed. More and more I reserve it to the time when it is conspicuous by its absence. It hasn't really been absent. It has permeated everything to this point. But now it's time to bring it out of the shadow and into the light.

The Foundation

I don't distinctly remember the first time I came upon St. James' definition of religion. But I liked it. I still do. It's so crisp and clear. "Religion that God our Father accepts as pure and faultless," James writes, "is this: to look after widows and orphans in their distress and to keep oneself from being polluted by the world" (James 1:27). I like that. But Martin Luther didn't.

That should come as no surprise. Luther's 16th-century concern was faith, not works. He felt that the weed whacker of "right belief" was what was desperately needed to rid life's underbrush of what he called "dead works." Not so with St. James. He did not see his day's primary religious problem as flawed faith, but puny works. James argued, in great detail (James 2:14–26), that if there are no works there is no faith. It's not that works are more important than faith. The two are partners. But in James' day the partner most likely to be dozing was works. It needed awakening and he jostled it to bright-eyed alertness.

The years passed and flowed into centuries. The focus of discussion on the faith/works dialog rotated. By the 16th century a belief in the importance and power of works had overwhelmed any proper understanding of the crucial position of faith. That's the world Luther came upon—and the reason he found James' writings so unappealing. Unappealing? An understatement. He called the Book of James "a straw epistle" and would have deleted it if he could.

So who's right? James? Luther? For the most part, unless you want to get into a "which came first the chicken or the egg" argument, the best Christian answer is, "Both, with one or the other's view in the forefront, depending on the struggle of the moment." In Luther's historical moment the distorted doctrine that needed clarification was how we are saved. Questions about faith dominated the religious discussion of his day. Were I living then I would have stood where the reformers stood. But, this is not the 16th century—not the 17th, 18th, or 19th either. We live on the far edge of the 20th century, about to slip over into the 21st. A lot of committed Christians think the dominant religious problems of our day are more related to James' concerns than Luther's. Christians seem overwhelmed with problems of how to live the life in Christ. For them the faith questions are settled. The creeds summarize what, and in whom, they ought to believe. The strain comes in living as our acknowledged Savior, the Son of God, taught.

That is the view taken by both the Christian teachers and the effective parents who described their views. For them the tension area *for Christians* has shifted from confusion about faith to a bewilderment about works—about what we do *after* we have received God's gift of faith. Such as a proper Christian stance on abortion; or the use of all kinds of drugs; or the unequal distribution of wealth; or medical care for all; or pregnancy-preventing pills; or whether the terminally ill may abbreviate their lives; or a view toward crime and its prevention; or fair housing laws; or racial and gender inequalities; or our responsibility toward homosexuality and lesbianism; or premarital and extramarital sex. In listing these few examples I haven't touched bioethical questions such as gene splitting, organ transplants, the use of fetal tissue in medical experimentation, artificial extensions of life for the elderly, our view of DNA, and more. The world in which we "live and move and have our being" (to use the language of Luke) is not Luke's. No matter what position some theologians take in the faith/works debate, the letters from effective *Christian* parents make very little mention of faith. Nor do the *Christian* teachers offer much on that subject. And when I look back on my years of ministering to Christian families as a parish pastor, faith, in the Reformation-era sense, was seldom on the agenda.

But why? If it was such an important subject then, why does faith surface so seldom in the remarks of the very people who were taught to put it on the highest pedestal in the first place? I have a simple answer. Faith is assumed. It is a given, like the pilings driven deep into the earth under a skyscraper which are so essential, but unseen. The reason works—what we do because of what we believe—are so prominent is that the finger is pointed at our inability to *apply* what we believe.

That assessment, accurate though it may be, creates problems for me as a Christian. Granted that faith may be a given for many, I know it is not so for all—not even all professing Christians. Whenever they are my audience, I stick with Luther, and insist that James' concerns are not the most important. For that reason if anyone reading this book does not possess God's gift of saving faith, don't go any further without asking Him to give you His greatest gift: faith. If you don't know how to ask for faith, repeat these words,

Lord, I have an incompleteness, an emptiness, that I yearn to be filled. I have been told

You revealed that need to me through Your Spirit and have given me a sense that there is more to life than what I know. I am also told that anyone who asks for Your gift of faith will be satisfied by You early. I ask, give me what I do not yet have: a faith that trusts in Your sacrifice of the Savior for me and that accepts what You have done for me through the redeeming blood of Christ. I ask this in Jesus' name, and for His sake.

That's a seeker's prayer which God will hear—and answer. He will! It, in turn, will open the door to the action that always follows saving faith. So say our "expert" consultants on faith-in-action, both teachers and parents. For depositions on how faith translates into action we turn to those elementary schoolteachers who make their point fast.

Model for your children. Actions speak louder than words, writes one.

Another plows into the James/Luther, works/faith controversy with, *Show your love for the Lord by your actions*. Anything vague about that?

A third expands on those two Christian encouragements with, *Show your love for Jesus by how you talk, worship, and live in your home*. Short, sweet, and to the point.

They press the point that faith, to be faith, moves into action. The "pure religion" concern of St. James is religion-in-the-heart that has moved to religion-in-the-hands. Faith becomes works. It happens so fast that for all but the theological technicians the two are always seen as one. In the language of car makers, faith and works are "unibodied"—all of one piece. They hold hands, always. Teachers say that.

Now the tough part. Having expressed the ideal, how do we pass on to our children this understanding of the linkage of faith and works? "Simple," the teachers respond. While the doing is tough, they assert that the understanding is passed to children as parents (1) *show* their faith in action before their children and as they (2) publicly *model* their faith through godly behavior. That's what teachers say.

Simple? Not really. Not simple, at all—not unless love, and care, and truth, and fairness, and a hundred other ingredients of the full life are simple. The ways we pass on the compound of faith-in-action is by involuntary "showing" and "modeling." Once our heart is set on Jesus, what we do is unconscious reaction. Our children, sitting in the front row for our demonstrations of what we believe is best in life, see our round-the-clock showing-modeling. We are never offstage to them. We are constantly in the spotlight.

Our teachers want to do more than offer generalized comments about modeling and encouragement to try. They want to be specific in the hope that their experiences will help both your children and you. So they offer a short list of practical things to do. All the items are basic.

They begin with an interplay of the words *action* and *reaction*. One good teacher observed: *Parents often model more for their children by their reactions than their actions. Kids read more into how parents react to a situation than what a mom or dad later says, or does, about it.*

Whew! Modeling by reaction—what a fascinating observation! Looking back on my life, first as a child and then as a parent, that pithy comment hits the nail right on the head.

Our children have told me that when I'm not pleased I "set my mouth." I assumed my facial expressions in family moments were benign, controlled, neutral. I *never* intentionally signaled my feelings or tried to dominate by veiled messaging. So thought I! The kids don't agree, nor does my wife who laughs her concurrence. They allege that I do, and have been for years, trying to control and shape without saying a word. I have heard of fathers who dominate the dinner table with their glance, and mothers who control with a slight turn of the back or tapping of the toe or a quick intake of breath. I wonder if they are as unaware of their *re*action as I was? The bad thing is that these subtle reactions inhibit communication. (And all the while I thought I masked my first feelings so well! Evidently I was the only one fooled.)

There are other avenues of reaction that are not so delicate and coy. Some are very heavy-handed, with an accent on the third, fourth, and fifth letters of the word re*act*. It shows its face as verbal abuse and physical abuse—sometimes both. But it's not the component out of which discussion, reflection, nurturing, or learning happens. Oh, yes, there is learning: A child "learns" not to try that topic with a mom or dad again. Sudden and oppressive action gets results, all right—but not the results a caring parent is after.

But, enough negative. I'm not interested in illustrating what's wrong or demonstrating the inappropriate. Who needs lessons in flawed modeling? The destructive skills come so naturally. The need for guidance lies on the positive side—on the constructive modeling that teachers, supported by hundreds of effective parents, urge us to offer our children. Joined in their suggestions by effective parents, our teachers offer four ideas on how you can help your grade school child succeed in school and society. Don't let their simplicity fool you. All four are profound and express essential qualities of life.

Model 1: Let your children see you love, care for, and respect your spouse.

If the home is a stage (and it is), it isn't a very large one. There's not much going on that isn't observed by everyone. Teachers are amused when parents tell things their children "don't know" about home activities. Don't know? They know everything, and what they don't actually see they feel. For six months I lived in a house in which the children worked overtime trying not to catch their mother smoking. She was so sure and so proud that her children didn't know she was addicted to cigarettes. The home is really a tiny theater with all corners visible to everyone.

There aren't that many roles either: Mom, Dad, Daughter, Son, Brother, Sister, maybe a Resident Relative. That's it. It doesn't take anyone long to learn all "the parts" that go with each role. I remember getting exasperated with a badly dysfunctional family I was counseling. Not knowing what to do, I asked everyone to rise, move over one chair, sit down and then assume the role of the person they replaced. The mother became the father, the father became daughter number 1 who became number 2, who became the little brother. And the little brother became the Mom. Guess what! Once I started the conversation again, it flowed without a hitch. Everyone knew everyone else's lines so well they could deliver them right on cue. I'm not sure things are that different in my home, except we present better roles and teach finer lines.

Home is an ideal place for helping a child pick up the basics of life, particularly when teaching the essentials is intentional. Note that last word: *intentional*. That means there ought to be a plan. All you have to do is make a short list of the skills and qualities that are essential to the kind of person you want your child to be. Then model those skills/qualities with your spouse. Let the child hear you affirm them in your partner; show affection to your partner for practicing those skills/qualities; and encourage and support them in your partner. What your children see at home is what they take to school and translate into how they treat others.

It's really not very complicated. The best way to teach honesty is by being honest with your life partner before your children's eyes. Same goes for respect, care, concern, helpfulness, love, and honor. Children catch these qualities from you. They treat others in school the way they see things lived at home. And, you know, the way they treat their classmates largely determines how others will treat them.

Within the broad category of things parents teach their children, our elementary school educators zero in on one specific that is absolutely fundamental in life.

Model 2: Forgive your child—in so many words—and then live as if your forgiveness is genuine.

Forgiveness doesn't have a lot to do with forgetting at first. It has to do with remembering and, after their confession, choosing to apply the appropriate meaning of the word forgive: (a) cover over, (b) let go, (c) send away. You do not forgive your child for what they have done to someone else. That's a decision for the other. You forgive your child for what they have done to you: the embarrassment you suffered through their conduct, or the hurt you felt by the way they rejected your teaching. Those are the areas in which your forgiveness is appropriate and needed. When the child asks for forgiveness, give it. You might even say, "I would like to forgive you for what you have done, and I will—when you ask." Forgiveness that is offered without confession cheapens the meaning of the word. Besides, it is useless, for the unconfessed sin remains unforgiven. Confession and forgiveness set the stage for putting the matter behind the both of you. But first, you and your child must act. As a penitent, your child will want to confess. You will want to forgive. Then comes the forgetting.

Once you have "covered over" a mistake, or "sent away" a hurt, or "let go" an anger, the forgetting just happens. There is encouragement enough in the Bible to do one or all of the three, even in the most painful of circumstances. Our teachers are assuming you will want to do that. So what's their newer insight? They suggest two additions to your act of forgiving: Say it out loud and then live it.

I never cease to be amazed by how many people—parents, partners, friends—explain very patiently, as if you are a slow learner, "I don't have to tell my wife/child/friend that I have forgiven them. They know it." Oh, do they? Then why is there so much misunderstanding in the world of family and friends on that very subject? Why do spouses wonder and children worry? You *do* have to tell them. If you don't, they are left to guess—and they are just as likely to guess wrong as guess right. Given those choices, why not speak up?

Some hesitate to speak words of forgiveness because they aren't ready to risk the forgiving life. The forgiving life is built on the idea of giving forgiveness as a gift. Love is a gift. Trust is a gift. A second chance is a gift. Friendship is a gift. All these gifts imply a risk. The risk may be that the other may reject, abuse, despise, or ignore your gift. That's the chance you take. Chances like that add spice to life. You can never be sure what the other will do. Their response is out of your control. But yours isn't. It's very much in your control and, as such, is one of the great teachers of life. How we remember what another did for us when we didn't deserve it! How we remember when we were forgiven! There's no better way to learn the importance and power of forgiveness than by being forgiven. That lesson lies within your power to teach. In addition to everything else, it's a gift-lesson that keeps on giving. It gives to you today and keeps on giving to your child— and through your child to others, for years to come.

And to think: This can be done at home— by you—for your child!

Model 3: Find ways to reach out and help others. Do it in the sight of your children, and let them be a part of your serving.

I have a heart for missions. It was shaped within me by my parents. As a child my mother and father lived the mission spirit before my very eyes. Because of them, I believe today that it is important to share with the less fortunate. Why? In the 1930s my parents gathered everything, from Sunday school lessons to clothing, for our poor brothers and sisters (that's how they were described to us) who lived on Indian reservations or were downtrodden by segregation in the South. Walter, Betty, Audrey, and I often walked to Sunday school because Dad used to pick up children whose parents were willing to let him do what they were unwilling to do. I could spin out a dozen more sentences like those three. But they are enough to capture the model of our mom and dad. They acted out their convictions and allowed us to participate in them at whatever level we were willing and able. My brother, my sisters, and I have tried to be copies of our parents.

Teachers have a strong commitment to the see-and-do approach to training a child. They are backed, with powerful intensity, by the effective parents. But how do you follow their advice? Woven into their letters the teachers and parents offer many examples. Here are a few:

1. Do volunteer work and take your children with you, especially in doing things like packing food and clothing at Christmas, Easter, and Thanksgiving. Your children will never forget those days!

2. Be a door-to-door solicitor for one or more of the great funds that seek support each year. Let your children join you. You and they will get to know a lot more people in your neighborhood. The likelihood is that they will learn about your community's generosity. And if that's not how it turns out, they'll learn about the meaner side of the human spirit too.

3. Get involved in a hands-on project such as Habitat for Humanity. Check the social service agencies in your community for other projects that can use your support. And, of course, take the kids.

4. Do something as basic as phoning for organizations such as Disabled American Veterans or Goodwill. Tell your child what you are doing—and why.

5. Watch newspapers for announcements of community clean-ups, special projects, marathons, and so many other things. Make one or more of them a family project.

Once you get into the flow of your community's serving organizations, you will find out about more that can use your help. And there are the various scouting organizations, 4-H, FFA, school-related organizations, Big Brother/Sister, and Little Leagues without number. There are so many ways to "show" how you feel about serving others. Almost all of them are open to help from your children as well.

But for Christians there is a unique unifying family activity that will bless everyone.

**Model 4: Excitement about worship
and giving develops in the
child who sees parents joy-
fully worshiping and giving.**

Any question in your mind that the child
reflects the parent? Certainly not in the mind of
our teachers. This is particularly apparent in the
world of worship and the practice of faith. If it
is important to you that your children mature as
practicing and positive Christians—and it certainly was to Audrey and me—nothing enhanc-
es that more than a family worship style that
emphasizes the excitement of praising God. In
the home in which I was raised, and in the
home in which Audrey and I raised our children, Saturday night was a night of focus aimed
at getting ready for the fun of Sunday. Church
was an extension of our home, the place we
publicly practiced what we privately practiced.
In describing the world in which I was raised
and in which we reared our children, I am not
lifting up an exception. It was—and is—the
norm in millions of fine Christian homes.
Believe me.

And what happened when the family fal-
tered in its ideals? What happened when sin
came into our home? We practiced all the ideas
and ideals mentioned in this book to this point:
We talked. We listened. We forgave. We taught.
We helped each other. We tried to practice a
lovely suggestion which one teacher presented.

She said: *Show them Christ's presence in the ordinary and everyday, rather than isolate Him to Sunday morning.*

How can there be dullness about the day when so many great things are celebrated: the resurrection of Christ, the completion of creation, the great Pentecost coming of the Spirit, the Christian's day off! That's what Sunday is. If we have all that straight, we will import the glory of that day into Monday and the days following. As a matter of fact, that's one of the things Christian homes do best. They take the extraordinary wonder of Sunday and infuse it into the ordinary all week long. They do this in so many different ways that no one book could ever contain them all. Go at it. Seek the wonder of God in the everyday. Do it hand in hand with your child. Neither of you will ever regret the effort or forget the experience.

This chapter isolates those things the teachers consider foundational matters. The basics. Core concerns. Things that are at the root. There are not so many that we are overwhelmed with detail. Each comment is offered for your consideration and, I hope, implementation. Do the best you can. No one calls you to perfection, only to faithfulness in effort coupled with forgiveness for failures. That takes us back to James—and Luther. Now, which is the more important? Neither. Both.

Application

The toughest thing about writing a sermon is the application. The application focuses on the area of life the sermon fits or the way it ought to be lived. A lot of preachers never get to the application. They find an amen before they get there and never finish their Sunday morning task. If they do that often enough, people catch on and stop coming—or come with such low expectations that they might as well stop coming.

This condition is nothing new. Alfred Lord Tennyson took a critical look at preaching a century ago through the poem, "Ode to a Northern Farmer." He spoke the mind of many about pointless preaching in the dialect of a simple English country man who described a sermon he had just heard. He wrote:

"I 'eard 'im a-bumming away like a buzzard cock ower me head,

And I niver knowed what 'e meaned, but I thought 'e 'ad summat to say,

And I thought 'e said what 'e ought to 'a said and I coom'd away."

I have not modeled the writing of this book after the poor and pointless sermon Tennyson described. I've tried to make specific suggestions page after page. This book is full of comments that count. Some are by elementary schoolteachers. Some by effective parents. Some flow from my experiences. All of them are practical, down to earth, and pertinent. If you have been reading with pencil in hand, I'm sure you have noted many suggestions that will control the dizziness of your child's elementary school days.

But there is a more intentional way to make this book useful. Sure, parents want guidance in dealing with their children's day-to-day problems. Those concerns are important. But to really power through the elementary school days and move into the high school years with assurance, a more comprehensive approach is needed—one that is not as focused on answers as on how life's better answers might be found. Not every family faces the same problems—or the same problems in the same intensity. What's needed is a way of finding good, homemade answers that fit the needs of your home. If that is what you have been after, look no further. This chapter is what you seek. In the hands of caring parents, it's an introduction to a whole new way of handling life. If it were a college course, it might be called Saving the Family through Problem Solving 101.

Want to enroll in that course with me? I hope so. You'll never regret it. But first, there's a two-part readiness test to pass. Part 1 is a question: "Are you a caring parent who wants to see your child gain all that's best for them?"

Go ahead and pick yes. Why else would you have read this far? You obviously want the best for your children. To make sure, look into your heart for the answer. What do you see? You tell me—better yet, tell yourself. I've already told you what I think.

Part 2 is another question. "Do you believe family problems can be solved?"

I say yes, for you—and hope you agree. Granted, few problems are solved as quickly as we would like or in exactly the way we project. But when Saving the Family through Problem Solving 101 is activated, a wide span of relational riddles are regularly resolved. And it's done in a much better fashion than most had ever hoped, leaving benefits which most had never imagined. This mechanism helps you identify good answers to family conundrums, and it energizes you to claim them. A spirit of expectancy permeates the life and spirit of those who know a way to solve problems and who consistently apply the one I am about to share.

So, are you ready? I hope so. But ready or not, here we go. I'll walk through the course outline, moving from question to question, using these questions as stepping stones from parenting uncertainty about family predicaments to parenting relief in finding a way.

Question 1: What's the issue?

Most home explosions are caused by a confusion about what's the issue. It's the Tower of Babel, all over again. Remember that story in Genesis 11 in which folks lost their capacity to communicate? The story isn't farfetched. It happens every day. Let me sketch an instance of multiple and conflicting issues at work within a simple family event.

Third-grader Lilah came home from school happy as a lark to tell her mother that she was invited to her classmate Laura's birthday party. Mom's answer: "You won't be able to go ... " and she gave a reason involving going to Grandma's on that very day. Oh, the stunned reaction of Lilah! She could hardly speak and her eyes glistened with tears.

Her sixth-grade brother, Kevin, got home about the time the flow started. He jumped right in—on Lilah's side. Ten minutes later Lilah's senior-high sister, Abby, walks through the front door. She also backed the birthday party. So it was three against one by the time Dad drove up and was immediately drawn into the discussion. Not sure of what was going on, he supported his wife.

Supper was a miserable experience. But, why? I know. Ignoring the fact that parents and children disagreed, the real culprits (note the plural) never were mentioned. A little digging will show us that other forces were stirred when Lilah came home with her happiness. Let's start with Lilah.

For Lilah the party was irrelevant. She just wanted to be with Laura and friends for three reasons: (1) Laura was the most popular girl in her class; (2) Lilah's best friend Lynn, who seemed to be spending more time around Laura than Lilah liked, was going; (3) She heard that in the past those who attended Laura's birthday parties received wonderful gifts from Laura's parents as they left. Lilah's yearning to go was urged by social instincts, a bit of jealousy, and plain old greed. She never mentioned all that. She just looked abused and cried.

Kevin would have backed Lilah no matter what. He would have backed her for two reasons: (1) He was angry with his parents for the two-week grounding he was serving because he went to the mall without permission; (2) In family conflicts the three kids had begun sticking together about a year ago; they found they could handle their parents better that way. No one had stated it that clearly, but it was a fact.

Abby had additional reasons for supporting Lilah: (1) She was convinced her parents didn't understand what it was to be young today; (2) She had "mothered" Lilah from the day she came home from the hospital and naturally protected her.

Mom: (1) Worried that Laura's home was way above their home, and she would look bad by comparison; (2) There really was some kind of vague plan for visiting Grandma—sometime; (3) She didn't know how she could reciprocate the invitation.

Dad was looking out for number 1. He had been burned once this month already. Without consulting his wife he had grounded Kevin, a punishment with which his wife did not agree—and in the privacy of their bedroom her coolness had let him know how she felt. He also believed that kids were pampered and got too much. They weren't being raised as he was. And, finally, he believed Lilah was spoiled and needed to learn she couldn't always get her way by crying. The tears were a final reason for supporting his wife.

And all that over an invitation to a birthday party! Now, what was the issue—were the issues—at work when Lilah came home? So many things intruded on this little event. That family had any number of unresolved issues lurking in the background, issues that apparently had never been surfaced one-by-one and discussed. Totally apart from Lilah and her needs, this family could use a meeting at which the concerns of each member could get a hearing. At the very least, a lot of the side issues would be identified and isolated. And who knows how things might have worked out then? The way things were going now, no one would be a winner. The saddest thing is that they wouldn't even know why they lost.

So, what's the point? This: Before you can "settle" an issue, you must first identify and define it. All must know what it is. In doing that, the ultimate decision may not change, but the family spirit and home dynamics sure will. As a first step in solving any family problem, you must determine to make no decision *until the issues are defined to the satisfaction of all concerned.* That's not difficult. All you need is a time together marked by openness (so people will talk), attentive ears (so all can hear), and a willingness to work together. Is that asking too much? Whether it is or not, no family gets anywhere in their life together without it.

Question 2: Having defined the issue, what are our choices?

Defining issues is not an end in itself. Its purpose is to set the stage for making choices. Every issue has at least two choices imbedded within—a good solution and a bad one. More often than not, there are many more choices— many more good ones and many more bad ones. Except in matters of clear moral choice circumscribed by God's Word, families are free to choose their responses to a defined issue from a wide span of alternatives. There really are many different ways to skin a cat, as the old adage states.

As an example, the incident with Lilah was filled with many short- and long-term choices, options which no one exercised. Mom could have chosen to listen and defer a response. Lilah could have obeyed. The older brother and sister could have stayed out of something they did not understand. Or support Mom. Or serve as interpreters. The husband could have been a model of a responsible parent and partner. And that is just the first level of choices. But they went out the window when all decided to protect their own turf by responding impulsively. Of course, if all had been sure their concerns would be dealt with, they might have reserved judgment and waited. Many families have the practice of regular family meetings, which any of them can call. But not this family—which is yet another undefined issue.

Crucial to claiming this vital step of identifying choices as a part of a successful problem-solving method is the recognition that there are always choices. Always. Take the time to look for them. In family matters check out whether it's possible to go to Disneyland via Washington, D.C., at the same cost; weigh all the reasons for a driver's license at 16; discuss the many band instruments your son might want to play; glean lots of information about sailboats before the family decides which to buy. Do all this especially with elementary school children who are so ready to learn the better ways to handle things and would be so happy to learn about them with and from you. Choices, folks, gather the choices. Do it *before* you move to the third question. It's the scary one.

Question 3: How will the choice be made and who will make it?

You're in a family, right? Looking down the road of life it is evident that the family which now exists will not endure. Children will grow. Parents will age. Relationships will change. The same little bundle of uncontrollable energy who tears all over the house will someday be your C.P.A., advising you on investments. How he will feel about you then and, more important, what kind of person he will be is directly related to your understanding about who has a part in the decisions—put another way, who makes the choices.

You are making a bad mistake if you say, "Hey, wait a minute! My kids are 9, 12, and 17. I'm not trusting them with anything serious!" My great-grandfather and some other 10-, 11-, and 12-year-old boys were entrusted with all the community livestock when Quantrell's

Raiders (his most famous [infamous?] follower was Frank James, brother of Jessie) came looting down the river bottoms of southwest Missouri during the Civil War. Those "kids" took all that could be moved out onto the prairies and guarded it while their moms and dads stayed home to defend the homestead. An exception? Read about the age at which David faced Goliath—and the dumb adult advice that almost dumped the whole deal—in 1 Samuel 17. And then check out the age of midshipmen in the British navy for most of its history and the role of drummer boys in all our wars up through the Civil War.

My point? Kids are competent. Given a chance they will prove it. Given teachers they will learn. That's why the whole family ought to have a piece of all the action. Even if you ultimately are unable to honor their guidance (which grew out of your training), at least get their views. Hear their comments and count their votes. Keep the final action in your hands. That's the parentally correct thing. But walk with them toward the goal of their full participation in the process. What better gift to your children than being able to say, "I appreciate your careful consideration and am ready to follow your advice." In those dozen words you have blessed them for life. Remember: Within two decades after their birth, they will be making decisions on marriage, college, career, life goals, and so many other things *without your input,* unless you teach them a better way—consultation and shared decision-making.

And if they want to do something that most normal folk could not honor, let them down easy. Honor their effort. Explain the different direction you feel you must determine upon reflection. Respect their effort. Then move on to the next moment which they can share. But before you do that, make sure you are finished with this one.

How? Get some action going based on your (their) decision.

Question 4: How do we put legs under our finding?

Somewhere on the road between the deciding and the doing most good ideas expire. Actually they are just abandoned, left to languish along the highway of good intention. They are as hopeless as beached whales. Good ideas need activation, implementation, and energy if they are to live. So the fourth question which Saving the Family through Problem Solving 101 faces is an action question: "What do we need to do now?"

To show you what I mean, let's go back to Lilah's excitement about the birthday party. Suppose that once the dust had settled the family decided their problem was that each was living in his or her own world, forgetting what it means to be a family. I can see them reaching that conclusion, given all the hidden hungers and hurts each one brought to that moment. And I can imagine them developing a range of reasons for their shouting matches, including the recognition they were not teaming much. I can see some emotional admissions of fault and even see them hugging each other as they expressed their determination to change. I can see all that. Can you?

Regrettably, it's very possible that the moment won't last. Hardly a week will pass before another family member's issue throws the family into an uproar again. And why? Were the family members hypocritical or insincere? No, the problem is that they didn't finish the job. They built half a bridge, and half a bridge is no bridge. Decisions, once made, must be implemented—fully. Only then will the family will be given form and life.

Suppose that instead of making tearful promises to do better and then heading off for bed, one of the family members had recalled a wonderful weekend they had shared at a campground 200 miles away. And suppose that after considering other choices, they all agreed that over the next long weekend the family would pack up the camping gear and revisit the past. That decision is better than doing nothing, but it's barely half a bridge. And it will stay that way until dates are set and duties are assigned. Mom needs to find the first long weekend everyone is available. Kevin needs to check out the camp gear. Abby can reserve a camp site. And Dad better get the car in shape and see if the trailer hitch has all its parts so that the camping trailer makes it all the way. Lilah? Bring the games, the guitar, and the songbooks. And Mom, probably, ought to figure out the supplies—with Lilah's help. And someone else ..., and someone else ..., and someone else .... And, finally, someone needs to make a checklist making sure that all the individual actions are taken. Kevin? That's what it means to put legs under a decision.

It's not always as complicated as the example. But this is for sure: If specific assignments are not made, little or nothing will happen and the dividing will start again.

Question 5: How are we doing?

Once you get moving there needs to be specific times to stop and evaluate. What happens if Lilah discovers many of the game pieces are lost and, besides, no one likes to play those games any more? And what happens if Dad discovers the camper trailer is badly rusted, the hitch is broken, and the family has grown so much that they don't fit in it anymore? And what happens if Abby finds out the old campground has been sold and is now a resort? Then what?

It could be a time to give up. It could be. It could also be a time to talk about all the other things you had in mind when you decided to do things together. You may discover that tastes have changed. Or interests are not the same. Maybe it's as simple as people have grown. New possibilities offer themselves. With all that whirring around in the family mix, you have before you a glorious opportunity to go to the next question.

Question 6: Should we go back and start again?

Just asking the question gets you back in the loop and on your way down this six-step sequence. Of course, you go back and start again, but it's not in the same place. Since you stood at the second question, trying to define the issue, there have been lots of changes. You have changed. Those around you have changed. Your understanding of the issues has changed. The choices have changed. Everything has changed. That changing is what puts the daze in school days. Parenting is a continuous beginning as you use the method outlined in this chapter to help your family deal with all the issues developed from page 1 to here.

Talking with caring teachers and with effective parents has given me such a lift. The world seems to believe that neither exist anymore. They clump them together with dinosaurs and other exotic creatures of the past who are now extinct. Don't you believe it. They *do* live and move and have their being and, in addition to everything else they say, want you to know you can be like them—effective parents guiding effective families. No *perfect* parents or *perfect* families. Real families who bless each other with all that God has given them as they stand under the blessings of the cross.